Social Competence and Social Skills

Zilda A. P. Del Prette • Almir Del Prette

Social Competence and Social Skills

A Theoretical and Practical Guide

Springer

Zilda A. P. Del Prette
Department of Psychology
Federal University of São Carlos
São Carlos, São Paulo, Brazil

Almir Del Prette
Department of Psychology
Federal University of São Carlos
São Carlos, São Paulo, Brazil

ISBN 978-3-030-70126-0 ISBN 978-3-030-70127-7 (eBook)
https://doi.org/10.1007/978-3-030-70127-7

This Springer imprint is published by the registered company Springer Nature Switzerland AG
The registered company address is: Gewerbestrasse 11, 6330 Cham, Switzerland

Preface

Social skills, which are required for successful interactions, have been considered as a protective factor for development, health, and well-being, and on the contrary, interpersonal problems are recognized as risk factors for this. Evidence concerning these relationships seems to be the main interest regarding the topic of interpersonal relationships.

Coinciding with this interest, we have observed a growing movement of theoretical, practical, and research fields concerning social skills in Brazil over the last two decades. Theoretical, because any scientific discipline requires theories that explain the human functioning within the scope of the topics it privileges. Practical and research, because applying available knowledge is supported by advances in scientific research.

This manual is part of this movement and is the result of knowledge accumulated in recent years about social skills and social competence. It is divided into three parts, sequentially organized to: (I) address the theoretical basis that guides and justifies decisions of interventions in this area; (II) provide information on procedures, techniques, and intervention resources regarding the logic of social competence requirements; and (III) present practical guidelines for planning and conducting programs to promote social skills and social competence in both group and individual formats.

In Part I, Chap. 1, after briefly describing the field of social skills, contextualizing the concepts of social skills and social competence, we aim to define social skills and their main classes and subclasses, as well as their nonverbal and paralinguistic components (NVPC). This is followed by a proposal of a social skills portfolio (including these components) aiming to organize deficits and resources as the basis for defining intervention objectives that meet clients´ needs.

In Chap. 2, the focus is on the renewed analysis of the concept of social competence, understood as strategically central in relation to the others. Criteria are defined to evaluate social competence, highlighting the instrumental and ethical dimensions of this construct and its implications for interpersonal relationships. Thus, a social competence model is proposed that includes four components: (1)

variability in social skills, (2) self-monitoring and contingency analysis, (3) knowledge and self-knowledge, and (4) ethics and values of coexistence.

Chapter 3 addresses the notions of interpersonal tasks, social roles, and cultural practices as contexts relevant to understanding social skills, social competence, and also client deficits and resources to deal with interpersonal demands. The aim of this discussion is to highlight the possible contribution of social competence to outline new cultural practices in different sectors of human coexistence.

Chapter 4 presents the rationale for social skills training (SST) programs based on the positive correlations and problems associated with social skills deficits and other requirements of social competence. Regarding these considerations, a brief presentation is made on preventive, therapeutic, and professional programs, as well as on the possibilities of interventions in group and individual formats. At the end of this chapter, we present the rationale of the experiential method, defining experiential activities and their use for promoting social skills and social competence.

Part II presents guidelines for promoting social competence and its requirements. Chapter 5 focuses on the evaluation (initial, process, continuous, and final), highlighting the importance of evaluating the follow-up of the results obtained. From this perspective, the evaluation instruments and procedures usually used in Brazil are briefly presented. In Chap. 6, practical guidelines are presented to use experiential activities and other procedures, techniques, and resources involved in promoting social competence. Chapter 7 addresses, one by one, the requirements of social competence, providing guidelines on how to promote them, using the intervention conditions described in the previous chapter.

Part III deals with planning and conducting programs to promote social competence and its requirements in group and individual formats. In order to do this, after considering structural and formal aspects of a program, we highlight the special care taken and guidelines to define the relevant objectives of intervention with clients, organization throughout sessions, and the planning of each session.

Based on previous analyses and information, Chap. 9 presents an intervention plan through an SST program. This plan is organized into files including suggestions of different activities, for example, homework, experiential activities of lead-ins to sessions, action plans for the three phases of each session (initial, intermediate, and final), and different procedures. Readers will also note that the group and individual formats are considered, each of them exemplified with a case study.

Chapter 10 includes 27 activities (experiential activities and practical exercises), tested for SST programs and referred to in the files presented in the previous chapter. Each one is described in detail, considering: (a) objectives, (b) materials, (c) procedure, (d) observations, and (e) variations. They are experiences and new activities in relation to others already published by the authors.

São Carlos, São Paulo, Brazil

Zilda A. P. Del Prette
Almir Del Prette

Acknowledgments

This manual is the result of many years of study and research. We would like to take the opportunity to thank colleagues as well as graduate and undergraduate students for their valuable collaboration, not only in psychology, but also in psychopedagogy, education, and other areas.

We are grateful for the valuable contribution from our peers in the field of social skills who, in response to our request, have suggested various contents of a manual for a country still lacking in this type of publication. Suggestions from these colleagues were important so that the final result would cover, if not all, at least the main contents expected of a manual. Therefore, we would like to thank Ana Carolina Braz, Daniele Carolina Lopes, Camila Negreiros Comodo, Camila Pereira-Guizzo, Carolina Severino Lopes, Elizabeth Joan Barham, Sheila Giardini Murta, and Talita Pereira Dias. We would especially like to thank our colleagues Camila Negreiros Comodo, Shirley Simeão, and Talita Pereira Dias for reading Chap. 9 and making suggestions. We are still grateful to Jane Godwin Coury and Anik Setti for the careful translation of our book (original in Portuguese) into English.

As in other books, we would also like to affirm that this product is part of our commitments to the National Council for Scientific and Technological Development (CNPq), which supports us with productivity grants. We would like to mention our affiliation to the Federal University of São Carlos (UFSCar), as senior full professors, as well as the Graduate Program in Psychology (Zilda and Almir), Graduate Program in Special Education (Almir) and to the National Institute of Science and Technology on Behavior, Cognition and Teaching (INCT-ECCE, Zilda).

We would be grateful if readers could send us any comments about the book to the following e-mail addresses: adprette@ufscar.br and zdprette@ufscar.br. Readers will be able to find articles on the topic addressed in this book at our website: http://www.rihs.ufscar.br, available for downloading, as well as summaries and reviews of our books.

Contents

List of Figures

List of Tables

Part I
Conceptual Basis

Chapter 1
Social Skills

Abstract After briefly describing the field of social skills, we aim to define social skills and their main classes and subclasses, as well as their nonverbal and paralinguistic components (NVPC). We discuss the relation between the topography and the functionality of social skills. This is followed by a proposal of a social skills portfolio (including these components) aiming to organize deficits and resources as the basis for defining intervention objectives that meet clients' needs.

Keywords Social skills · Social competence · Nonverbal · Paralinguistics · Repertoire portfolio

The term social skills is used with two meanings. The first, which is broader, indicates a theoretical and practical field in which psychological knowledge is both produced and applied. The second, which is more restricted, refers to one of the key concepts within this field. In this chapter, the term social skills will be first discussed as a theoretical and practical field and then later on as a concept and how it relates to social competence, which is central to other concepts in the field.

1.1 Social Skills as a Theoretical and Practical Field

The field of social skills has been in development since the mid last century and draws from several different theoretical approaches in psychology. Dating back to its origins, knowledge produced from cognitive, behavioral, and sociocognitive psychology can be highlighted (Del Prette & Del Prette, 1999). In Brazil, behavioral analysis and cognitive behavioral approaches have especially contributed much conceptually, empirically, and practically to knowledge production in the field of social skills since the very first studies. These contributions appear in different axes of knowledge production, as illustrated in Fig. 1.1.

Various reviews from the Brazilian literature in the field, at different periods of time (Bolsoni-Silva et al., 2006; Freitas, 2013; Fumo, Manolio, Bello, & Hayashi, 2009; Murta, 2005; Mitsi, Silveira, & Costa, 2004; Teixeira, Del Prette & Del Prette,

Z. A. P. Del Prette, A. Del Prette, *Social Competence and Social Skills*,
https://doi.org/10.1007/978-3-030-70127-7_1

Fig. 1.1 Knowledge production axes on social skills and social competence

2016; Del Prette & Del Prette, 2019), show that production in social skills, in each one of these axes, has grown considerably, especially more recently. Historically, theoretical essays have relied on research about social interaction, social behavior, interpersonal relationships, and, later, nonverbal communication (see Argyle, 1967/1994). Nowadays it can be said that theoretical studies precede and follow empirical research, focusing on issues relevant to the development of the field from different conceptual perspectives.

1.2 Social Skills as a Concept

As a concept, it is important to highlight the historical controversy concerning the relationship between social skills and social competence. At times, these terms are understood as conceptual equivalents, at others as irreducible to one another and sometimes as complementary.

The differentiation between social skills and social competence started with studies conducted by McFall (1976/1982), who argued in favor of the distinction between them, including their practical ramifications. Although this distinction is not a consensus in the area, it is adopted by many researchers and theoreticians, such as O'Donohue and Krasner (1995), Trower (1995), and Gresham (2009), among others.

The choice of recognizing and making the conceptual differences between these terms explicit, as in this manual, dates back to the first Brazilian studies (see Z. Del

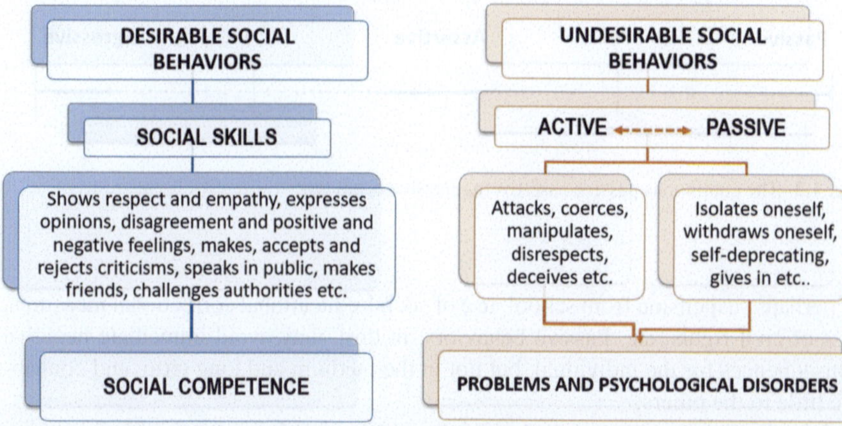

Fig. 1.2 General schema of the social behaviors classes concerning the concepts of social skills and social competence (A. Del Prette & Del Prette, 2001; Z. Del Prette & Del Prette, 1999, 2005)

Prette & Del Prette, 1996, 1999). Thus, the centrality of the concept of social competence in relation to the other concepts in the field is proposed. It is expected that the importance of this decision, both for understanding and applying concepts and for planning and conducting Social Skills Training programs, will become more understandable throughout this manual.

The diagram below shows the relations between these two concepts and the classes of socially competent behaviors considered desirable and undesirable in social coexistence.

As shown in Fig. 1.2, roughly speaking, social behaviors can be divided into two categories: desirable and undesirable. In most cultures and subcultures, socially competent behaviors considered desirable are those guided by values that include mutual respect between the interacting individuals; those considered undesirable are those which contradict these culturally shared values. The criterion that determines desirability is based on the consequences of each behavior in terms of benefits and harm caused to the interlocutor, the group, and the community, as well as, in many cases, their acceptance by the culture.

Accordingly, the left column lists some socially competent behaviors that will later give rise to the classes and subclasses of social skills and thus can contribute to socially competent interactions. The column on the right represents socially undesirable behaviors, which can be either active ("antisocial") behavior or passive (nonsocial) behavior. In the first, problematic behaviors are externalized, and in the second, problematic behaviors are internalized; they are generally associated to psychological disorders and may require clinical intervention and/or referral to the legal sector and psychosocial healthcare services.

Active undesirable social behaviors often produce immediate satisfactory results for the individual but at the cost of negative results for the interlocutor, as well as the group and the community. They can also incur reprisals and the end of a friendship

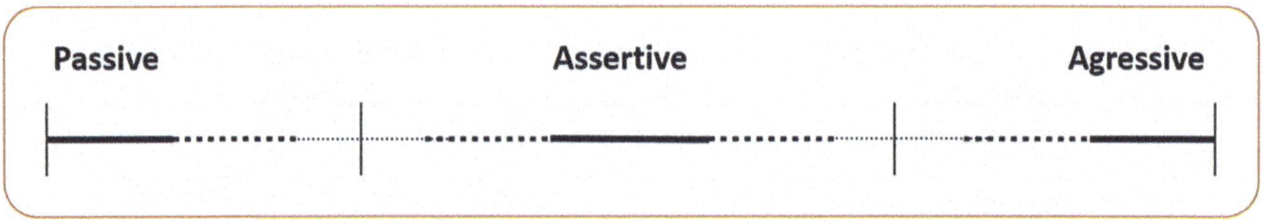

Fig. 1.3 The continuous passive-assertive-aggressive behaviors

or perhaps suspension from school, use of social-educational correctional measures, loss of civil rights, etc. Passive behaviors, in turn, may avoid immediate negative consequences for the individual, but not in the medium and long term, and contribute little to the others.

It is also important to remember that passive and active patterns of behavior are not fixed but occur within a continuum, as shown in the illustration proposed by Del Prette and Del Prette (2003) when discussing assertive patterns (Fig. 1.3):

It is important to mention that both desirable and undesirable behaviors are maintained because they allow an individual to either generate positive consequences or avoid negative consequences for themselves. This is why behaviors that compete with desirable ones are considered, as they result in consequences that are obtained from undesirable behaviors rather than being obtained from the desirable ones. Thus, while the undesirable ones are strengthened, the probability of learning and desirable behaviors occurring is reduced. Despite this simplified scheme, the complexity of the determinants concerning problematic behavior and other psychological disorders cannot be overlooked, but only the role of consequences is highlighted, which can be the target for educational and therapeutic interventions.

An aggressive but successful demand competes with an appropriate, polite request and may reduce the probability that an individual emits the correct behavior in the future.

1.3 Definition of Social Skills

The concept of social skills is reasonably intuitive, and, perhaps for this very reason, an operational definition for it is especially necessary, thus avoiding errors and directing both practice and research. What, then, are social skills, and how does one differentiate between the different types, or classes, of social skills? How is context important to socially skillful behavior? These and other questions are important to fully understand this construct.

As a concept, the term social skills applies to a set of social behaviors that share specific characteristics. An adequate definition for this term must include at least three interdependent characteristics.

Social Skills refers to a *descriptive* construct ① of social behaviors valued within a certain culture ② that have a high probability of bringing favorable outcomes to an individual, their group, and community ③ that can contribute to socially competent interactions during interpersonal tasks.

This definition identifies the so-called social skill behaviors and differentiates them from passive and active, undesirable behaviors associated to disorders and externalized and internalized problems, respectively (Del Prette & Del Prette, 2005). Behaviors categorized as social skills can contribute to social competence for they produce the desired outcome for social interaction (this may be, e.g., successfully making a request and having it fulfilled, expressing disagreement and being respected in one's right to express opinions, or asking a question and receiving an answer, etc.). It is important to point out, however, that social skills can contribute, but do not necessarily result in social competence, for this includes other criteria, aside from social skills, as will be discussed further on.

By definition, the concept of social skills indicates a general domain of social behavior and its subclasses. Thus, the adjectives *skillful* and *unskillful* should be avoided so that they are not mistaken for the concept of social competence, which will be discussed in the next chapter.

1.4 Classes and Subclasses of Social Skills

Behaviors characterized as social skills can be found in the literature grouped into sets called domains and subdomains. What does classifying behaviors mean? It means grouping them based on some feature they share that differentiates them from the characteristics of other groups. This is no less true for social behaviors, which may be classified by their topography (formal aspects of behavior, such as gestures, tone of voice, facial expressions, body language, etc.) and functionality, that is, their effective function in a given situation, considering the threefold relationship of contingencies (antecedent-behavior-consequence).

The diversity of functional classes of social skills, that is, social behaviors that have the same function, can be exemplified with the domains of empathy and assertiveness. The domain of empathy brings together expected and desirable social behaviors in relation to the interlocutor, especially when he or she is experiencing some kind of difficulty. In this case, the objectives are to support, demonstrate understanding, validate feelings, etc. On the other hand, the domain of assertiveness joins together expected social behaviors in situations of imbalance in interpersonal exchanges, disrespect, or threat of loss of rights, with the function of restoring the previous condition or improving the current condition, characterizing itself as coping, as it involves a risk of an undesirable reaction of the other (A. Del Prette & Del Prette, 2001). This function is shared by the subdomains of assertive social skills, such as arguing, disagreeing, questioning, refusing, etc.

Any skill may be taken as a broader domain when the purpose is to examine its components. A domain may be decomposed to the extent that subdivisions are no longer identifiable units of social skills.

Within a class, behaviors have similar functions but may present different topography. For example, the class of civility includes behaviors of greeting, thanking, saying goodbye, etc., all with similar general functions in the culture but differentiated regarding topography. Behaviors grouped in the class of civility, such as greeting, thanking, saying goodbye, etc., have the function of *adjusting to standards of politeness*. If we take the behavior of greeting someone as an example, it can be observed that it presents rich variability in topography. Someone can wave at another, hug him/her, or shake hands. All these variations do not prevent them from being categorized as a greeting; in other words, they share the same function. Choosing the appropriate topography depends on the subculture to which those involved in the interpersonal task belong.

On the other hand, some classes may have some of its subclasses in common with another domain. For example, asking/answering questions and expressing feelings are embedded in both the domains of assertiveness and empathy but with differences in the topography that characterizes each of them. Consider asking/answering a question when faced with a demand for assertiveness and a demand for empathy. The difference is in the volume, speed and tone of voice, in the facial expressions, gestures, and different characteristics of eye contact.

There is still much to research about the categorization and classification of social skills, both in conceptual and empirical terms. Just to exemplify this, A. Del Prette and Del Prette (2009a) analyzed possible conceptual correspondences between the classes of social skills defined in that field and those classes of verbal operants identified by Skinner (1957), discussing two separate taxonomies for social behaviors.

1.4.1 General Social Skills Portfolio

In addition to their conceptual classification, social skill classes and subclasses can also be refined by empirical evaluations. Therefore, any taxonomic proposals (classification proposals) cannot be viewed as definitive structures nor as proposals consensually established in the literature of the field. Even so, having access to a good classification system can make it easier to identify a client's deficits and resources to orient an assessment and promote the social skills relevant to different clientele. The organization of these domains (both resources and deficit) can be called a social skills portfolio.

Social Skills Portfolio: it consists of a list of domains and subdomains of social skills relevant and pertinent to tasks, social roles, and the developmental stage of a client, including NVPC.

Considering the main social skills that have been the object of research and practice in our environment, we can organize them under the different axes of analysis (Del Prette & Del Prette, 2008). Throughout the developmental stages, the individual is met with interpersonal demands variety of classes and subclasses of social skills. Table 1.1 shows the main classes of social skills identifiable in the literature that may be relevant to all stages of development and to the social roles assumed throughout them.

These ten general classes of social skills and their respective subclasses are recognized as relevant throughout the life cycle. The proficiency expected for each domain can vary according to the age and stage of development of an individual and may become even more critical, or relevant, during certain stages. For example, a young adult will be better at receiving criticism than a small child. Even considering the peculiarities specific to their developmental stage, however, both should present some of the main behaviors in the domain when dealing with criticism. There are other social skills that are expected to develop only at a certain stage, such as those related to dating and sex in adolescence. Others, though they may occur in any developmental stage, are accompanied with differing expectations regarding the proficiency and complexity of the behavior (such as speaking in public or coordinating groups).

1.4.2 Basic Social Skills

Among the social skills classes presented in Table 1.1, some could be considered as basic social skills, as they are found in several domains. Therefore, they should be learned or honed by all participants in an SST. What are these skills?

Basic social skills include observing and describing behaviors, recounting interactions, asking and answering questions, giving compliments, etc. These classes should be improved as early as the initial sessions of a program, as well as those of giving feedback, carrying out contingency analysis, and demonstrating positive affection, because, besides facilitating subsequent acquisitions, they contribute to structuring a therapeutic context of participation and support between clients, significant individuals, and therapists.

Table 1.1 Portfolio of social skills classes

1. **Communication.** Initiate and conversation, ask and answer questions, give and ask for feedback, give and accept compliments, state opinions, remember events; communication can occur directly (face to face) or indirectly (through electronic means); during direct communication, verbal communication is always associated with nonverbal elements, which can complement, illustrate, replace, and, at times, contradict the verbal message
2. Civility. And/or respond to greetings (when entering or leaving a room), use the words *Please*, *Thank you*, and *I'm sorry*, and follow other standards of politeness of a culture, discriminating their diversity and nuances
3. Making and maintaining friends. Initiate conversations, share information freely, exchange confidences, demonstrate kindness, maintain contact without being invasive, express emotions, give compliments, provide feedback, respond to contact, send messages (email, notes), invite and accept invitations for outings, make contact on festive occasions (birthdays, Christmas, etc.), express solidarity when faced with problems
4. Empathy. Maintain eye contact, approach another person, listen (avoiding any interruptions), adopt another's perspective (put yourself in someone else's shoes), express understanding, encourage trust (if applicable), show willingness to help (if applicable), share the other's joy and fulfilment (birth of a child, getting into university, getting a job)
5. Assertiveness. As is an ample class with many subclasses, the most important are highlighted below: ✓ Defend your own rights and those of others ✓ Question, consider, disagree, request explanations about the motives for certain behaviors, express opinions, agree, disagree ✓ Make and refuse requests ✓ Express anger and displeasure and request changes in behavior ✓ Apologize and admit mistakes ✓ Deal with criticism: (a) accept criticism (listen attentively until the interlocutor finishes), ask questions, request clarifications, look at the interlocutor, agree with the criticism in its entirety or in part, apologize; (b) criticize (speak in a clear, audible tone of voice, maintain eye contact without being intimidating, state the reason for the conversation, show the other one's error, ask for a change in behavior; (c) reject criticism (listen attentively until the interlocutor finishes, maintain eye contact, request a turn to speak, give your account of the facts, express opinion, relate your rejection of the criticism to the truthfulness of the facts) ✓ Talk with a person who has a role of authority: greet, introduce yourself, state the reason for the approach, ask and answer questions, make a request (if applicable), make a note, schedule a new contact (if applicable), thank, say goodbye
6. Expressing solidarity. Identify the needs of the other, offer help, express support, engage in socially constructive activities, share food or other objects with those who need them, cooperate, express compassion, take part in meetings and solidarity campaigns, visit those in need, console, motivate colleagues, and make donations
7. Managing conflicts and solving interpersonal problems. Calm down by exercising self-control when faced with the emotional indicators of a problem, recognize, name and define the problem, identify those behaviors belonging to oneself and to others associated with the continuation of the problem or its solution (how they evaluate it, what they do, what is the motivation for the change), devise alternative behaviors, propose options for changing behaviors, choose, implement and evaluate each alternative, and combine them when necessary

(continued)

Table 1.1 (continued)

8. Expressing affection and intimacy (dating, sex). Approach and demonstrate affection to the other by eye contact, smiling, touching, asking and answering personal questions, freely sharing information, recounting events of interest with the other, incentivizing a good mood, sharing jokes, demonstrating kindness, making invitations, showing interest in the other's well-being, dealing with intimate and sexual relationships, setting boundaries when necessary
9. Coordinating groups. Organize activities, distribute tasks, encourage everyone to participate, control time and focus of the task, give feedback to everyone, ask questions, mediate interactions, set goals, compliment, paraphrase, summarize, require the completion and quality of tasks, explain and request explanations, check comprehension about problems
10. Speaking in public. Greet, glance at the audience, use an audible tone of voice, modulating it according to the subject, ask/answer questions, direct attention to audiovisual aids (read the necessary minimum), use humor (if applicable), recount personal experiences (if applicable), report events (include subclasses from the previous item), thank the audience for their attention when finishing.

1.5 Social Skills: Topography and Functionality

The social skills described in Table 2.1 comprise verbal elements (what is said), but their effectiveness depends greatly upon their shape of behavior (manner in which it is said). Thus, analyzing resources and deficits in a client's social skills should take into account the nonverbal and paralinguistic components (NVPC) that characterize the form or topography of performance and refer to aspects such as posture, facial expression, eye contact, fluency of speech, etc.

> Changing the topography is critical because it affects behavioral functionality.

Regarding social skills, topography and function are closely related. Small changes in behavior (facial expression, posture, gestures, tone of voice, etc.) can often facilitate or affect its functionality or, in other words, its results in interpersonal tasks (A. Del Prette & Del Prette, 2009a). The functionality and effectiveness of social skills, therefore, cannot be considered independently from their topography or shape, i.e., from NVPC (A. Del Prette, & Del Prette, 2009a).

The importance and diversity of the NVPC in the field of social skills have been described in the literature (A. Del Prette & Del Prette, 1999; Caballo, 2003; Z. Del Prette & Del Prette, 2009b). Figure 1.4 shows the main items for NVPC, which should be object of attention during SST programs.

The items in Fig. 1.4 must be evaluated by the therapist and added to the client's portfolio. Some authors (Caballo, 2003) include within the NVPC physiological indicators (blushing, tremors, etc.) and outward appearance (clothes, accessories,

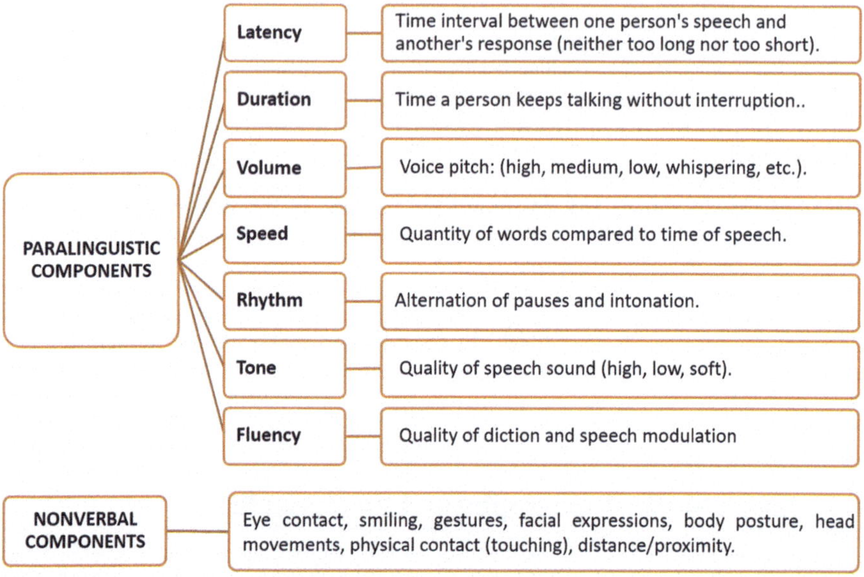

Fig. 1.4 Portfolio of nonverbal and paralinguistic components

makeup, etc.) since they can have an impact on the evaluation of social competence. There is an extensive knowledge production about the NVPC, especially by Argyle (1967/1994, 1984). Based on this research, there are some important considerations to be made for the SST program.

- NVPC can support, emphasize, and complement the meaning of the verbal communication; in some cases, they may even contradict it, for example, when someone says they are fine and simultaneously show a thumbs-down gesture.
- People generally have good control over *what* they say but less so over *how* they say it, especially regarding motor extremities. For example, they may have a serene facial expression while they drum their fingers on a surface or swing their legs continuously.
- Given the difficulty in controlling NVPC of behavior and their association to the physiological alterations typical of emotional states, they are often more reliable indicators of feelings (and sometimes beliefs) than the content verbalized through speech.
- Just as with any other social skill, the evaluation of NVPC should take into account the culturally accepted patterns for each situation or interpersonal task.
- Generally speaking, adequate NVPC situates themselves between low and exaggerated expressiveness. Some examples of problematic behaviors are excessive eye contact (staring) or insufficient eye contact, speech that is too fast or too slow, excessive or no gesticulation, etc.
- Gestures can assume completely diverse or even opposite meanings in different cultures.
- Some typical NVPC patterns may include cultural differences related to gender: acceptable for women, but not for men, or vice versa (Fig. 1.5).

Fig. 1.5 Basic expressions of emotions

In face-to-face interactions, verbal content (what is said) is always accompanied by the nonverbal and paralinguistic components of communication (how it is said). With the advent of virtual communication, the challenge is to communicate feelings through writing. Even using punctuation marks established in the language (exclamation and interrogation marks, suspension points, etc.) that allow the identification of a *subtext* or *reading between the lines* of a written message, it seems necessary to have available extra emotional indicators by using graphic symbols. This is why emoticons and other illustrations used as complements to a written message are increasingly more explored, for they can better transmit emotions, intentions, thoughts, etc. Therefore, the question of topography can also be applied to virtual interaction mediated by writing.

1.6 Learning Social Skills

Many individuals' needs are mediated by other individuals and depend on interactions between them. This is a characteristic of any social behavior, in a common environment (Skinner, 1953), in which the behavior of one person can be an antecedent to or consequence of the other's behavior. Thus, social skills are also social behaviors. And as any behavior, social skills were and are the result of three processes of variation and selection: the phylogenetic, ontogenetic, and cultural processes (Skinner, 1981).

Phylogenetic selection refines anatomical, physiological, and behavioral characteristics favorable to the acquisition and perfecting of those social behaviors, among which are social skills, which lead to survival of the species (Trower, 1995). Taking Glenn's analysis of verbal behavior as a base (Glenn, 2004), Del Prette and Del Prette (2010) highlight, among others, the following characteristics: flexible facial muscles, refining facial expressions, and the discrimination of stimuli derived from the other's expressiveness during the social interaction, sensibility to social stimuli and the tendency to approach others belonging to the same species (gregariousness), and susceptibility to selection by consequences, increasing the possibility of learning in relation to others.

Ontogenetic selection refers to those social skills learned over a lifetime. This learning occurs mostly in natural conditions, present in families, at school, work and leisure environments, etc., and through three interdependent processes: modeling, instruction, and learning by consequences.

In terms of cultural selection, the influence of culture on social skills is already widely recognized. Each culture establishes which social behavioral patterns are valued, tolerated, or disapproved, from among those disseminated among its members and reproduced over time. Considering that culture is never monolithic, and that it encompasses different subcultures, certain behaviors accepted and expected in some subgroups can be rejected in others and vice versa.

In summary, as with any other behavior, social skills (and the remaining requirements for social competence, discussed in the next chapter) are learned over time through formal and informal processes and interactions with other people. They are, therefore, influenced by culture and the immediate contingencies of the environment. When the natural environment is not favorable, difficulties and flaws during acquisition and honing of social skills may occur, possibly involving problems with competing behaviors, whose overcoming will require educational and/or therapeutic interventions. These interventions basically involve restructuring the aforementioned learning processes, this time in favorable conditions.

References

Argyle, M. (1967/1994). *Psicologia del comportamiento interpersonal [The psychology of interpersonal behavior]*. Madrid: Alianza Universidad (1967 original).

Argyle, M. (1984). Some new developments in social skills training. *Bulletin of British Psychological Society, 37*, 405–410.

Bolsoni-Silva, A. T., Del Prette, Z. A. P., Del Prette, G., Montagner, A. R., Bandeira, M., & Del Prette, A. (2006). Habilidades sociais no Brasil: Uma análise dos estudos publicados em periódicos [Social skills in Brazil: An analysis of studies published in journals]. In M. Bandeira, Z. A. P. Del Prette,& A. Del Prette (Orgs.), *Estudos sobre habilidades sociais e relacionamento interpessoal [Studies about social skills and interpesonal relationships]*. (pp. 1–45). São Paulo, Brazil: Casa do Psicólogo.

Caballo, V. E. (2003). *Manual de avaliação e treinamento das habilidades sociais [Social skills training and assessment manual]*. São Paulo, Brazil: Santos.

Del Prette, A., & Del Prette, Z. A. P. (2001). *Psicologia das relações interpessoais e habilidades sociais: Vivências para o trabalho em grupo [The psychology of interpersonal relationships and social skills: Experiential activities for groups]* (1st ed.). Petrópolis, Brazil: Vozes.

Del Prette, A., & Del Prette, Z. A. P. (2003). Treinamento assertivo: Ontem e hoje. [Training assertivity: Past and present] In C. E. Costa, J. C. Luzia, & H. H. N. Sant' Anna (Orgs.), *Primeiros passos em Análise do Comportamento e Cognição [First steps in the analysis of behavior and cognition]* (pp. 149–160). Santo André, Brazil: ESETec.

Del Prette, A., & Del Prette, Z. A. P. (2009a). Componentes não verbais e paralinguísticos das habilidades sociais [Nonverbal and paralinguistic components of social skills]. In: A. Del Prette, & Z. A. P. Del Prette (Orgs.), *Psicologia das habilidades sociais: Diversidade teórica e suas implicações [The psychology of social skills: Theoretical diversity and its implications]* (pp. 147–186). Petrópolis, Brazil: Vozes.

Del Prette, Z. A. P., & Del Prette, A. (1996). Habilidades sociais: Uma área em desenvolvimento [Social skills: A developing field]. *Psicologia Reflexão e Crítica, 9*(2), 233–255.

Del Prette, Z. A. P., & Del Prette, A. (1999). *Psicologia das Habilidades Sociais: Terapia, Educação e Trabalho [The psychology of social skills: Therapy, education and work]* (1st.ed.). Petrópolis, Brazil: Vozes.

Del Prette, Z. A. P., & Del Prette, A. (2005). *Psicologia das habilidades Sociais na Infância: Teoria e Prática [Psychology of social skills in childhood: Theory and practice]* (1st. ed.). Petrópolis, Brazil: Vozes.

Del Prette, Z. A. P., & Del Prette, A. (2008). Um sistema de categorias de habilidades sociais educativas. [A classification system of educative social skills]. *Paidéia: Cadernos de Psicologia e Educação, 18*(41), 517–530.
Del Prette, Z. A. P., & Del Prette, A. (2009b). Avaliação de habilidades sociais: Bases conceituais, instrumentos e procedimentos [Assessing social skills: conceptual basis, instruments and procedures]. In: A. Del Prette, & Z. A. P. Del Prette (Orgs.), *Psicologia das habilidades sociais: Diversidade teórica e suas implicações [The psychology of social skills: Theoretical diversity and its implications]* (pp. 187–229). Petrópolis, Brazil: Vozes.
Del Prette, Z. A. P., & Del Prette, A. (2010). Social skills and behavior analysis: Historical connection and new issues. *Perspectivas em Análise do Comportamento, 1*(2), 104–115.
Del Prette, Z. A. P., & Del Prette, A. (2019). Studies on social skills and social competence in Brazil: A history in construction. In: S. H. Koller (Org.), *Psychology in Brazil: Scientists making a difference*. Cham, Switzerland: Springer (ISBN 978-3-030-11335-3).
Freitas, L. C. (2013). Uma revisão sistemática de estudos experimentais no campo do Treinamento de Habilidades Sociais [A systematic review of experimental studies in social skills training]. *Revista Brasileira de Terapia Comportamental e Cognitiva, 15*, 75–88.
Fumo, V. M. S., Manolio, C. L., Bello, S., & Hayashi, M. C. P. I. (2009). Produção científica em habilidades sociais: estudo bibliométrico [Publications in social skills: Bibliometric study]. *Revista Brasileira de Terapia Comportamental e Cognitiva, 11*(2), 246–266.
Glenn, S. S. (2004). Individual change, culture, and social change. *Behavior Analyst, 27*, 133–151.
Gresham, F. M. (2009). Análise do comportamento aplicada às habilidades sociais [Analysis of behavior applied to social skills]. In A. Del Prette, & Z. A. P. Del Prette (Orgs.), *Psicologia das habilidades sociais: Diversidade teórica e suas implicações [The psychology of social skills: Theoretical diversity and its implications]* (pp. 17–66). Petrópolis, Brazil: Vozes.
McFall, R. M. (1976/1982). A review and reformulation of the concept of social skills. *Behavioral Assessment, 4*, 1–33.
Mitsi, C. A., Silveira, J. M., & Costa, C. E. (2004). Treinamento de Habilidades Sociais no tratamento do transtorno obsessivo compulsivo: Um levantamento bibliográfico. [Social skills training in the treatment of obsessive-compulsive disorder: A bibliographic survey]. *Revista Brasileira de Terapia Comportamental e Cognitiva, 6*(1), 49–59.
Murta, S. G. (2005). Aplicações do treinamento em habilidades sociais: Análise da produção nacional [Applications of training in social skills: Analysis of national production]. *Psicologia: Reflexão e Critica, 18*(2), 283–291.
O'Donohue, W., & Krasner, L. (1995). Psychological skills training. In W. O.'. Donohue & L. Krasner (Eds.), *Handbook of psychological skills training: Clinical techniques and applications* (pp. 1–19). New York: Allyn and Bacon.
Skinner, B. F. (1953). *Science and Human Behavior*. New York, Macmillan.
Skinner, B. F. (1957). *Verbal Behavior*. New York: Appleton-Century-Crofts.
Skinner, B. F. (1981). Selection by consequences. *Science*, 213(4507), 501–504.
Teixeira, C. M., Del Prette, A., & Del Prette, Z. A. P. (2016). Assertividade: Uma análise da produção nacional [Assertiveness: An analysis of national academic production]. *Revista Brasileira de Terapia Comportamental e Cognitiva, 18*(2), 56–72.
Trower, P. (1995). Adult social skills: State of the art and future directions. In E. W. O'Donohue & L. Krasner (Eds.), *Handbook of psychological skills training: Clinical techniques and applications* (pp. 54–80). New York: Allyn and Bacon.

Chapter 2
Social Competence

Abstract The concept of social competence is understood as being of central importance in the field of social skills. This premise is coherent with the definition of this concept, considering the evaluation criteria that derive from it, and coherent with the set of requirements at the basis of socially competent behavior. Criteria are defined to evaluate social competence, highlighting the instrumental and ethical dimensions of this construct and its implications for interpersonal relationships. Thus, a social competence model is proposed that includes four components: (1) variability in social skills (2) self-monitoring and contingency analysis, (3) knowledge and self-knowledge, and (4) ethics and values of coexistence.

Keywords Social competence · Social skills · Self-monitoring · Values of coexistence · Ethics

2.1 Definition of Social Competence

Most scholars from the field agree that the concept of social competence is vitally important to understanding the processes of interpersonal relationships. As a concept, the term social competence refers to the assessment of behaviors and the results of interactions; therefore, its definition should include at least the characteristics specified below.

> **Social competence** is an *evaluative* construct ① of an individual's behavior (thoughts, feelings, and actions) in an interpersonal task ② that meets the individual's goals and the demands of the situation and culture, ③ producing positive results according to instrumental and ethical criteria.

The definition presented emphasizes the evaluative character of social competence, applied to behavior (including coherence between public behaviors, accessible to observers, and private behaviors, accessible only to the person themselves)

Z. A. P. Del Prette, A. Del Prette, *Social Competence and Social Skills*,
https://doi.org/10.1007/978-3-030-70127-7_2

and the results of that behavior in interpersonal tasks, according to the individual's objectives and demands of the situation recognized in the culture. While the concept of social skills refers to the description of behavior in response to the question, *What did the participant do and how did he/she do it?*, the concept of social competence refers not only to the evaluation of the quality of this interaction but also to its effectiveness in terms of results, considering the interpersonal task. In the perspective adopted here, it includes answers to the following questions:

- What was the behavior like?
- What are the results of the individual's behavior?
- Were the results also good for the interlocutor?
- Can they also benefit both the groups to which the people interacting belong to and even the wider community?

In summary, assessing social competence implies considering the behaviors in the interaction and their immediate, medium-, and long-term results, not only for the individual but also for the other and the social group. These aspects are discussed in more detail below.

2.1.1 Social Competence: Private and Public Behaviors

In interpersonal tasks, a person's behavior depends on his/her social skills repertoire, but not only that. In most of these tasks, socially competent behavior requires articulation between various social skills and between those skills and cognitive and affective components, not directly observable, which include thoughts, feelings, objectives, patterns of achievement, self-efficacy, and self-rules, i.e., private behaviors associated with the interaction. Therefore, it makes sense to consider that a socially competent interaction implies being coherent between public and private behaviors and also in relation to the group rules in which the person engages and with which they agree.

Guided by an information processing approach, McFall (1982) includes, among the private components of social skills, processes to decode demands of a context (perception, interpretation, etc.), selecting and deciding about what and how to respond, as well as predicting possible consequences. These and other private components, which precede and accompany social behavior, are included in the concept of self-monitoring, which is considered an indispensable requisite for social competence and is dealt with in more detail in this chapter.

Coherence between public and private behavior is not always easily found in social life. It certainly occurs most easily when an individual's self-rules are coherent with the norms of the community in which they are inserted. However, the verbal community often positively reinforces public behaviors that do not correspond to private behaviors, such as misrepresenting or exaggerating facts, omitting events, and so on. In SST programs guided by values that benefit both interlocutors, it is important to establish conditions for the occurrence and strengthening of the correspondence between what one says to oneself (thinking) and public behavior in interaction with others, through specific procedures (A. Del Prette & Del Prette, 2001; Z. Del Prette & Del Prette, 2005, 2010) (Fig. 2.1).

Fig. 2.1 Coherence public-private actions

2.1.2 Social Competence Evaluation Criteria

According to Schlundt and McFall (1985, p.23), the attribution of social competence *involves a value-based judgment by an observer concerning the effectiveness of an individual's behavior in a specific task*. Effectiveness means desirable results, derived from the individual's behavior in an interpersonal task. But what would these results be? If desirable, for whom? These questions raise the need for *criteria* to evaluate social competence indicators.

> The evaluator can be an external observer and/or the person in the interaction.

Linehan (1984) proposed a set of criteria to evaluate the functionality of social behavior related to assertive behavior in women. The author advocated three criteria for considering assertiveness: achieving immediate goals, maintaining or improving the interpersonal relationship, and maintaining or improving self-esteem. Considering social competence (as a construct differentiated from that of social skills), these criteria were included among those proposed by Del Prette (1982, p.9), which added, at the time, that of *balancing reinforcers or, at least, ensuring basic human rights*. The set of criteria for assessing social competence (A. Del Prette & Del Prette, 2001; Z. Del Prette & Del Prette, 1999, 2005) is described as follows:

A. **Fulfilling the objective**. This refers to the specific and immediate consequences of the interpersonal task for the individual(s) being assessed and can be accessed in response to the question: Did the individual(s) meet the objective(s) of the interpersonal task?
B. **Maintaining/improving self-esteem.** This refers to the immediate consequences in terms of emotional indicators of personal satisfaction with the results obtained associated to the verbal community's approval, both helping to strengthen and maintain behaviors and to increase the participant's self-efficacy

in the interpersonal task. These consequences can be gauged in response to questions such as: *Has the interaction affected the self-esteem and satisfaction of those who took part in a neutral, negative, or positive way*?

C. **Maintaining/improving the quality of the relationship**. This refers to less immediate consequences in the medium or long term regarding interlocutors and the likelihood of maintaining or improving a positive relationship between them. Reflective questions help in the evaluation, for example, *Would both participants in the interaction seek new opportunities for social contact? Would one of the participants in the interaction avoid future contacts?*
D. **Balance of power between the partners**. This refers to positive reciprocal exchanges, whether of behaviors or concrete or symbolic products: *Did the interacting participants' behavior help to balance exchanges? Did they increase the imbalance, benefiting one person more than the other or to the detriment of the other?*
E. **Respect/amplification of interpersonal human rights**. This refers to the consequence of behavior in terms of human rights: *Did the participants' behavior help to maintain or extend socially established rights, for example, the right to be heard and taken seriously, to express opinions, to disagree, and to be respected in their dignity and physical or moral integrity?*

Some of these criteria are not easily applied but can be evaluated in their probability of occurrence, based on observing behavior and accounts. The first three (a, b, c) consider the immediate results and can be observed by those involved and by external assessors. The last three criteria include medium- and long-term results for those involved in the interpersonal task and, eventually, for the larger group. These results are not readily observable but can be inferred based on the report and knowledge of the norms and rules of the culture.

While the first criteria may be of more interest to one of the individuals, the latter must benefit the other and/or the group. Therefore, it can be affirmed that social competence criteria consider two dimensions of results: an instrumental, more immediate one that serves the individual interests of the interlocutors and an ethics dimension that can occur in the medium and long term, also attending to the interests of the social group (see A. Del Prette & Del Prette, 2001; Z. Del Prette & Del Prette, 1999, 2005).

It is important to recognize that, to be considered socially competent, behavior does not need to be exceptional but rather produce desirable results, according to the social competence criteria. As in many interpersonal tasks, not all social competence criteria are achieved simultaneously, and behavior can be evaluated as more or less socially competent, depending on the quantity and diversity of the criteria met. This relativity raises several questions:

- What is the essential or basic criterion for behavior to be considered socially competent?
- Can the individual who does not achieve his/her goals in interpersonal tasks be considered socially competent?

- If so, why would an individual whose behavior was assessed as socially competent not achieve his/her goal (Criterion A)?

These issues are related to the ethical dimension of social competence, which is included in the assessment criteria mentioned above. They are analyzed in more detail below.

2.1.3 Ethical Dimension and Basic Criterion of Social Competence

Some philosophers (Kant, in *Critique of Practical Reason*) assumed the existence of a moral law intrinsic to every individual, which regulated his/her actions. Irrespective of this possibility, legislators and governments sought to establish norms and laws that, on the one hand, punished undesirable behaviors and, on the other hand, made such behaviors unattractive considering their risks. However, these alternatives were also not sufficient to make social interactions free of imbalance, leading to significant losses on one side and gains on the other.

The law that emphasized punishment was called the law of talion. In ancient Mesopotamia, Hammurabi ensured that the rules laid down in various common cases in which he arbitrated were written on monoliths (large stones) and placed in visible places. However, negative reciprocity depended on possessions and prestige, and applying them penalized disadvantaged classes. This Code of Hammurabi was popularized by the popular saying: *An eye for an eye, a tooth for a tooth.* Much of the human legislation is still based on this code, and family and school educational practices also use it, even as they acknowledge its failure. In behavioral analysis, this cultural practice, still in effect, would be called *ceremonial*, according to Glenn (2005), because it benefits only those who are in control of the situation.

When analyzing the codes adopted in some ancient cultures, possibly against the law of talion, the so-called Golden Rule emerged. This rule can be found in various cultures (Jewish, Roman, Chinese, Greek) with small variations in the statements but maintaining the same meaning. In a simplified way, it establishes that one's social behavior is guided by *Do unto others as you would have them do unto you.* This rule could work as a discriminative stimulus for two or more people in interaction. It can also be said that, when the interaction begins, the individual who intends to be guided by such a rule estimates the impact of their behavior on others, supposing appropriate exchanges that benefit everyone. Following this norm seems to generate a high probability of positive reciprocity in the interaction, but not when the beneficiary is guided by another rule. Adopting the Golden Rule in cultural practices could certainly add to the so-called technological contingencies (Glenn, 2005), that is, those that are maintained for their usefulness in terms of results that benefit the group, in this case at least in terms of health and quality of life.

The reciprocity criterion, implicit in the concept of social competence, therefore, excludes behaviors that cause damage to others, emphasizing short-, medium-, and long-term results in terms of well-being for the interlocutor and the social group. This type of result characterizes what is called here moral or ethical values of coexistence, usually referred to as notions of justice, equity, freedom, solidarity, well-being, etc. It is based on the positive reciprocity of the Golden Rule that one can establish the basic or essential criterion for a behavior to be considered as socially competent.

It is understood that, for a *behavior to be considered socially competent*, it must meet the Golden Rule of *Do unto others as you would have done unto you*. Or, at least, *Not do unto others* as *you would not want done to you,"* thus avoiding negative exchanges and maximizing the likelihood of balanced positive exchanges between the interlocutors, with respect to interpersonal rights. This means that fulfilling personal goals that cause damage to others does not allow for a behavior to be considered socially competent.

Studies in the field of social skills have generally used only the instrumental dimension of social competence, possibly because the criteria for evaluating it are more easily accessed. However, in a study on bullying at school, Comodo (2016) demonstrated the possibility of investigating social competence indicators in victims, witnesses, and authors, producing results that, besides contemplating values of coexistence in school education, suggest procedures within some of the criteria of this construct.

Considering the criteria associated with the ethical dimension, it can be said that socially competent behavior supposes the possibility of choosing between courses of action. This choice is based on predictions of possible consequences, both for the individual and for others, in the immediate, medium, and long term. These choices require self-control, associated with ethical self-management (Skinner, 1968), in the sense of decisions about future courses of action and, therefore, analyzing possible contingencies in force (see Dittrich, 2010). Self-management, referred to here, as well as its ethical implications, refers to the concept of self-monitoring, as one of the requirements of social competence, described in the next chapter.

The possibility of choosing based on the contextual contingency analysis of the interpersonal task helps to answer the two final questions of the previous section: how and why an individual with a socially competent behavior in the B, C, and d and e criteria may not achieve their personal objectives in interactions (Criterion A). This can occur at least in cases where:

- Interpersonal tasks involve conflict between the participants' objectives in an interaction, such as a request asked competently that is refused by someone competent in the ability to refuse. For example, Julia makes a request to Marta and has her request declined. For Marta, who did not intend to meet the request, success in the task implies refusal. In this case, the most competent person can succeed to the detriment of the other. However, when the objectives are complementary, for example, in an interaction between a customer and a book seller, the social competence of one can benefit both interlocutors.

- Meeting the objective does not just depend on behavior, for example, an excellent job interview performance in a context marked by economic recession may not result in the intended goal of getting a job.
- The individual changes his/her behavior to ensure the other criteria instead of meeting the initial objective, in order to minimize damage and/or maximize positive results in the medium and/or long term, for example, to disagree with an interlocutor who demonstrates little emotional control.

In all the examples, achieving or not the desired results is an objective criterion, but not a sufficient one, as it does not include analyzing the contingencies of the interpersonal task (first example) and the broader context (second example), as well as the results for the interlocutor in terms of the ethical dimension (last example).

2.1.4 Social Competence and Reciprocal Exchanges

Adopting the centrality of social competence, when analyzing interpersonal interactions, requires two considerations. The first concerns the question of the balance of exchanges between the interlocutors; the second is related to the possibility of conflicting objectives in interpersonal tasks.

The momentary imbalance in reinforcing exchanges between members of the dyad or the group does not negate the importance of balance when one considers a longer lasting relationship. This balance is not static, but dynamic, with gains and losses that can alternate over time. It is this balance that increases the likelihood of maintaining relationships, for example, in affective exchanges between family, friends, spouses, colleagues, etc. Using the example of the marital relationship, the husband accompanies his companion in a sports event, when he would prefer to stay at home reading or resting. He does so by returning her kindness, who accompanied him at a commemorative meeting at the company where he works (Fig. 2.2).

Fig. 2.2 Exchanging in balance

These concessions characterize reciprocity in the aforementioned sense and require self-control, to renounce [a] or postpone immediate gains, seeking to maintain a pattern of positive exchanges in the medium and long term (Rachlin, 1974). It is also a question of overcoming egocentrism, as it is not always possible to maintain the intermittence of exchanges over time. In other words, exchanges are rarely immediate and giving in to the benefit of others occurs, over time, with alternating costs and benefits.

Of course, healthy relationships are formed not only from these *small acts of kindness* but also from the continuous exercise of empathetic and assertive communication. Experiencing different emotions, such as tenderness, joy, gratitude, love, friendship, etc., is part of long-lasting relationships. On the other hand, exercising assertive communication forms the basis for authentic relationships in the medium and long term. It is widely recognized that the immediate consequences of assertiveness may involve a cost to the two people interacting.

In summary, the balance of exchanges is dynamic, not static, i.e., it is not continuous and specific but a general and relativized assessment of exchanges that occur over time. Depending on the circumstances, this assessment can lead to three more likely alternatives:

1. Both parties obtain, simultaneously or alternately, similar benefits and costs.
2. One party gains more benefits than the other, which remains with higher costs.
3. Both parties obtain fewer benefits and higher costs.

Alternative 1 is certainly the most desirable but occurs less frequently. If the Golden Rule were applied (instead of the law of talion), alternative 1 would probably occur more frequently. Alternative 2 can lead to the relationship ending, which would be less likely when the imbalance is temporary or motivated by unavoidable events, such as prolonged illness of one of the members of the dyad, loss of relatives, unemployment, etc. Alternative 3 seems to predict a minimum survival of the relationship, barring exceptions such as the person who has a life of renunciation and accepts it as a kind of destiny.

Instrumental and ethical dimensions can be conflicting, especially in interpersonal tasks that characterize demands for assertive skills. In such cases, less developed social behaviors (passivity, avoidance, etc.) may occur, not due to deficits in social skills but in the individual's assessment of the likely negative consequences for the immediate or medium and long term. This is the case, already exemplified, of a person who does not state their opinion contrary to the position of another, perceiving that the person is emotionally fragile and that this could cause him/her even more discomfort at that moment (applying the Golden Rule).

2.2 Social Competence Requirements

Social skills are a necessary condition but not sufficient for social competence. One has to ask: *What are these other conditions*?

In addition to any organic dysfunctions, which could affect interpersonal behavior, and to have a good repertoire of varied social skills, several factors must be considered. Overall, the following may be listed:

- Finding results compatible with the social competence criteria in an interpersonal task, especially those associated to the ethical dimension.
- Identifying one's own resources and limitations, as well as the rules and norms of the social environment.
- Discriminating where, how, with whom, and at what time to respond to certain demands of interaction.

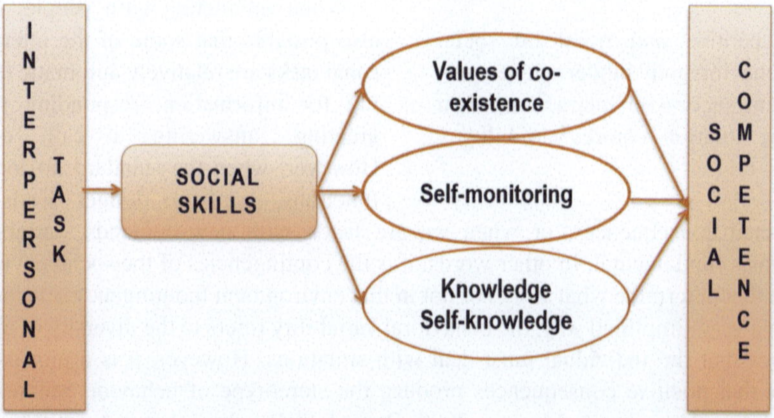

Fig. 2.3 Schematic illustration of social competence requirements

- Articulating skills in more complex behaviors by monitoring one's own *step-by-step* behavior.

These items point to other requirements of social competence that reinforce their differentiation from the concept of social skills. Thus, considering the concepts already presented, a didactic scheme can be proposed of the relationships between social competence and its requirements, emphasizing social skills, but including the others previously mentioned. This scheme is shown in Fig. 2.3.

According to the illustration, for an individual to be socially competent in a given interpersonal task, the individual needs to have four requirements: (a) a repertoire of social skills pertinent to this task; (b) commitment to values of coexistence compatible with the ethical dimension of social competence; (c) self-monitoring his/her behavior in the interaction; and (d) self-knowledge of resources and limitations, associated with knowledge of the norms and rules of the social environment in which they are in.

It is argued that encouraging these requirements is important in any Social Skills Training program that seeks results consistent with the concept of social competence. Each of these requirements is dealt with briefly and separately in the following sections, but all must be encouraged in an integrated way throughout a program.

2.2.1 *Social Skills and Behavioral Variability*

By and large, in most routine activities, including those of a social nature, people tend to repeat successful behaviors. This does not occur, however, for new and more complex interpersonal tasks. It can be said that in the usual interventions tasks, the required variability is minimal, and possibly unnecessary, as a stereotyped pattern achieves the expected results.

Repetitive and ritualistic social behaviors may hinder or even prevent successful interaction when the situation requires variability.

When interacting with people, it is also possible that some of the interpersonal tasks are relatively automatic (asking for information, responding to a greeting, answering a call, etc.). However, when the standard no longer functions, e.g., no longer leads to expected consequences, or when we are faced with new demands, variability becomes fundamental. In other words, it is the contingencies of the social environment that determine what works or not in that environment (contingency selection).

In a very simplified way, the behavioral variability refers to the diversity of alternatives that the individual must deal with situations. However, it is a mistake to think that positive consequences produce the stereotype of behavior. Studies on variability (Hunziker & Moreno, 2000; Rangel, 2010) show that it is not the reinforcement that produces the stereotype but the characteristics of the contingencies in which it occurs. In other words, repetition (stereotype) can be successful if the contingencies of the situation or interpersonal task require it (e.g., responding to a greeting, congratulating an acquaintance on his/her birthday, etc.). Although repetitiveness is successful, its limits should be considered, because in excess, it can be dysfunctional and be part of disorder indicators such as Asperger syndrome and obsessive-compulsive disorder. Cases of depression and shyness, usually recommended for SST, also require an emphasis on variability, increasing the likelihood of improving social skills repertoires.

Variability in topography may prove to be functional for certain demands. On the other hand, in repeated situations, variations in the topography of behavior can generate better results. For example, small changes in the tone of voice may characterize functionally different responses, altering behavioral effectiveness. Consider the possible differences between these two requests: (a) Do this for me! (ordering tone of voice); (b) Could you do this for me, please? (intonation for requesting something). They show differences between ordering and asking, suggesting, and imposing and may have different impacts on the interlocutor's response. However, in some situations, this is not enough to change just the topography: it is important to discriminate the demands of the situation and to change the social skills class over time or be prepared to deal with the demands of the situation.

Encouraging variability involves providing the participant with alternatives of social skills to address the relevant interpersonal tasks of his or her life. This variability can be conceived between and within classes, as shown in Fig. 2.4.

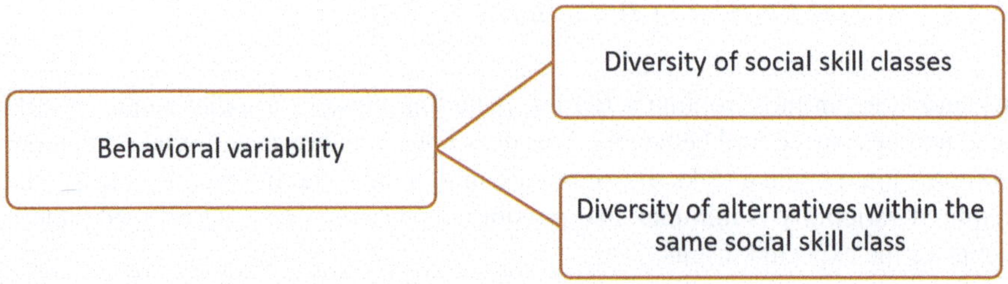

Fig. 2.4 Behavioral variability in SST programs

As shown in Fig. 2.4, variability can be encouraged both in terms of the diversity of social skill classes in the individual's repertoire (e.g., assertive, empathic, work, etc.) and in the diversity of alternatives (subclasses, topographies) within the same class (e.g., different ways of showing affection or assertiveness). In both cases, it is important to privilege those who are deficient and critical in their interpersonal tasks.

Variability is more than diversity of alternatives: it involves prior learning to discriminate task contingencies, choosing, testing, and evaluating potentially effective alternatives to deal with the demands of interpersonal tasks.

Variability is a basic condition for adjusting one's behavior to the objectives and demands of specific interpersonal tasks and also for adapting to changes from one social system to another. For example, starting school, participating in the adult world, starting a new job, etc., involve dealing with new, unknown, or unstable contingencies. Learning to discriminate contingencies does not often occur without direct exposure to situations and tasks, as well as to the consequences of each alternatives for dealing with them. In this case, instructional procedures do not often consider all the nuances of contingencies that signal relevant behavioral alternatives.

Exemplifying: after several successful interactions following instructions, a customer is faced with changes antecedent event and demands, which require behaviors that he/she has difficulty in discriminating. His/her alternatives are (a) to maintain the same behavioral pattern and (b) to not respond to the situation, avoid, and escape behaviors some way. However, the therapist recognizes that instruction, alone, without discrimination training, may not have the desired effects. In this case, other procedures could be more effective, such as (a) testing varied responses in some situations and maintaining repetitive patterns in others and (b) training the observation of negative consequences obtained by someone (film character) who maintains an unchanged response (without variation), when the situation requires change.

To sum up, it is understood that to be effective, an SST program focused on social competence should encourage variability and not merely the standardized training of social skill classes. Moreover, this variability must be linked to analyzing environmental contingencies and improving discriminate and sensitivity of the client to contingencies.

2.2.2 *Self-Monitoring*

In psychology, there are several definitions for the term self-monitoring. According to Dowd and Tierney (2005), for example, self-monitoring means *being aware of what you are doing*. This notion and other elements can be found in the definition elaborated previously by the authors.

Self-monitoring is a metacognitive and behavioral skill in which a person observes, describes, interprets, and regulates their thoughts, feelings, and behaviors in social situations.

Based on this concept and the literature on self-monitoring, Dias, Casali, Del Prette, and Del Prette (2019) specify the behavioral components involved in the process of monitoring one's behavior in interpersonal tasks. This analysis resulted in a list of behaviors (public and private) that could be considered as self-monitoring components, among which the following stand out:

- Recognizing one's own private behaviors (beliefs, feelings, self-efficacy, etc.) in a situation of interaction
- Identifying possible behavioral alternatives during an interaction
- Predicting likely consequences of different responses
- Choosing behaviors considering the alternatives available to them and their possible consequences
- Regulating the topography of their behavior during an interaction
- Exercising self-control in order to present certain behaviors and avoid others, based on assessing the probable consequences

To sum up, self-monitoring means observing one's behaviors, inhibiting impulsive reactions, predicting the impacts of different reactions, and changing behavior during interaction in order to take into consideration social competence criteria.

A very common example of self-monitoring occurs in health facilities. The attendant, realizing that the client has difficulty in hearing him/her, speaks a little louder and observes the result. If the customer shows that they can hear, the attendant maintains the volume of their voice, otherwise the attendant adjusts and checks the effect until checking that the customer shows they can hear.

Self-monitoring can be learned, initially in easier situations and those which are gradually more difficult. Self-observation is an indispensable condition for this and implies the ability to report one's own behavior, thoughts, and feelings. This capacity is related to the initial bases of self-knowledge. In a sense, one can conceive self-knowledge without self-monitoring; however, self-monitoring includes self-knowledge, since, during an ongoing interaction, to change one's behavior more effectively, the person must discriminate his/her own resources and environmental contingencies associated with different possible alternatives.

Parents and teachers of children, from an early age, request reports of behaviors and contingencies as a way to assess whether children still require more supervision. This procedure, even if unintentional, is a condition for the initial learning of self-monitoring. The child learns that their behaviors have consequences, and if it were other people, the consequences might also be different. For example, a child returns from his/her friend's house and the mother asks: *Who was at Arthur's house? What games did you play? Did Paula let you ride her bike? When she fell off her bike, what did you do?* (Fig. 2.5).

Fig. 2.5 Mother stimulates self-monitoring

Self-Monitoring and Sensitivity to Contingencies

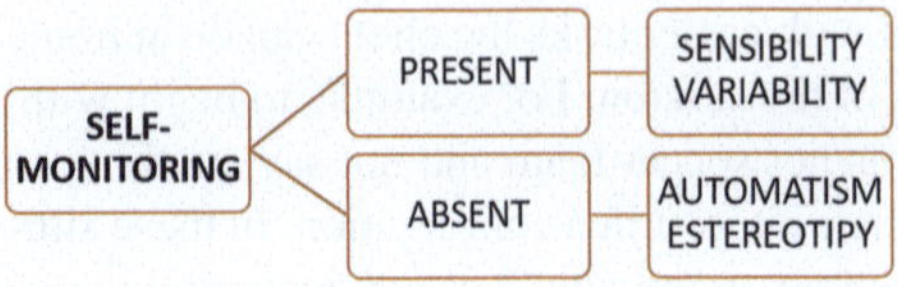

Fig. 2.6 Self-monitoring and sensibility

Self-monitoring is an important behavioral class to deal with interpersonal tasks, especially in the more complex ones. Its absence, in some interpersonal tasks, can strengthen stereotyped behavior that affects social competence. On the other hand, self-monitoring firstly depends on sensitivity to environmental contingencies, that is, discriminating and reacting to them. This is because, even if the person has an elaborate repertoire of alternatives likely to be positively reinforced, it is the contingencies in the natural environment that will select the most functional ones for certain situations and contexts. Self-monitoring, therefore, implies sensitivity and analysis of interpersonal task contingencies, as well as self-control to inhibit impulsive reactions and choose the best behavioral alternatives, as explained below (Fig. 2.6).

Self-Monitoring and Self-Control

Self-monitoring involves regulatory and decision-making processes that require self-control. Applying Rachlin's (1974) concept of self-control to socially competent behavior, it can be said that self-control consists of inhibiting impulsive responses, more likely but with immediate consequences that affect social competence, or resorting to the famous *marshmallow experiment* (Mischel, 1958), as the ability to tolerate gratification delay, that is, to replace answers that would generate immediate positive consequences for others with positive consequences only in the medium or long term. A good example is a person who reacts aggressively to a provocation (immediate response and more likely but with generally undesirable consequences) versus getting out of the situation or calming the other and asking them to change their behavior to solve the problem together.

From the very first months after birth, parents seek to teach self-control to their children. Although it is not considered a social skill class, self-control can be considered a basic condition for learning a set of social skills, among which are assertiveness, empathy, criticism, and solving interpersonal problems. Some difficulties of self-control are associated with competing behaviors, among them, outbursts of anger, compulsive lying, and tattling.

Encouraging self-monitoring sometimes requires self-control training. Some strategies for this may include the following tasks: (a) identifying more frequent situations in which *impulsive* responses occur and the consequences; (b) identifying situations in which the person has exercised self-control (even if with difficulty) and the consequences (positive and negative) verified; and (c) recording happenings and people before whom it occurred, or did not occur, self-control. For instance, relaxation workouts can also be included in situations that induce *negative* emotional reactions, cultivating *positive* emotions toward certain people.

Self-control training should be started with easier tasks the client can do at home and possibly with training in the context of the session. For example, to begin with, the client should hear peer jokes about his/her soccer team and not say anything or stop expressing opinion on a subject of their interest in a conversation. In these situations, one can also train the skill of listening attentively, looking, maintaining eye contact, waiting for the interlocutor to finish speaking, and only then asking pertinent questions or comments.

Self-Monitoring and Instrumental and Ethical Dimensions of Social Competence

Self-monitoring entails choosing between behavioral alternatives. Therefore, it can be related to both the instrumental dimension and ethical dimension of social competence. In instrumental terms, it is relatively simple to understand how observation, predicting consequences and regulating one's own behavior, helps the individual to obtain desirable outcomes. The issue is more complex in the case of ethical dimensions, as it involves choices based on predicting medium- and long-term results for oneself, for another, for the relationship, and for the social group.

Some studies have focused on the relationship between the field of social skills and the ethical dimension of social competence, considering the approaches that have contributed most to consolidating it: behavior analysis (Bolsoni-Silva & Carrara, 2010; Z. Del Prette & Del Prette, 2010; Gresham, 2009) and Bandura's social cognitive theory (Oláz, Medrano, & Cabanillas, 2017).

In the behavior analysis approach, the choices a person makes and the decisions he/she takes, which affect others, are referred to as an ethical self-management process (Skinner, 1968). This process implies behaving oneself based on the medium- and long-term consequences that can be foreseen. It therefore requires learning to estimate consequences as the basis for decisions consistent with the ethical dimension of social competence. Some challenges in this process are pointed out by Dittrich (2010, p. 53):

Perhaps the greatest tragedy in the world today is the low ability we humans have of predicting the consequences of what we do beyond our individual and immediate future. The emergence of qualities we generally call consideration and respect for each other depends, to a large extent, on the visibility we have of the consequences of our actions not only to ourselves but to others. To that extent, the consequence analysis may even be an educational resource.

The social cognitive theory (Bandura, 1986, 2008) also uses the concept of self-monitoring. Within it, the individual is an *agency* provided with an autosystem of processes that exercise a self-regulating function over their thoughts, feelings, and behaviors (Polydoro & Azzi, 2008). Self-regulation is characterized by processes that may be related to self-monitoring components. Regarding moral actions, self-regulation would selectively activate inhibitory mechanisms of self-censorship, restricting socially reproachable behaviors, as well as moral disengagement mechanisms that would generate justifications for adherence to culture-damaging behaviors (Azzi, 2011; Bandura, 2008). According to Bandura (2008), anyone is subject to the process of moral disengagement, which can be minimized by the development and commitment to ethical standards.

2.2.3 *Knowledge and Self-Knowledge*

For a socially competent interaction, it is essential to have knowledge (information) about (a) oneself, (b) the other, and (c) the context in which interpersonal tasks occur. The former can be referred to as self-knowledge. The other two are what is being referred to here as knowledge about the environment. This knowledge can be transmitted by language (narrative, explanations, descriptions, formulation of hypotheses, concepts, and theories) and/or inferred from the description of interpersonal tasks, their demands, and their contexts.

Knowledge About the Environment

As a requirement of social competence, the term knowledge is being taken in its generic sense of access to information about some relevant aspects of the social environment, such as the demands of the situation; subculture elements such as rules and contingencies; and possible convergences or divergences in the participants' interpersonal tasks. It is understood that the probability of contemplating the criteria of social competence increases with the knowledge about some aspects of the social environment that are relevant to a successful performance from the perspective of social competence. This knowledge, derived from previous information or from immediate and accurate observation, can describe, explain, and, to some extent, predict people's behavior. Relevant knowledge for socially competent interaction is summarized in at least two sets of information:

- Regarding culture: the norms and rules that regulate and define the social behaviors expected, valued, accepted, or disapproved for different situations and interpersonal tasks
- About the interlocutor(s): their probable social behaviors, objectives, feelings, and values of coexistence

Many social skills deficits and failures in social competence can occur due to not knowing which behaviors are tolerated, valued, and disapproved, i.e., the person does not know what to do or the possible consequences of different behavioral alternatives.

Self-Knowledge

Self-knowledge can be conceived as the ability to observe/describe one's own behaviors and to explain them in terms of possible associated variables (Skinner, 1974). This self-knowledge not only includes what is publicly accessible to others but also what is private, hidden, and slightly or not accessible to others. It is the case of beliefs, knowledge, feelings, expectations, self-regulations, etc. that, in Bandura's social cognitive theory (1986, 2008), are part of the individual's self-system, understood as an agency.

Self-knowledge is related to self-monitoring, but these concepts are distinguishable from each other.

Self-knowledge is an important requirement for self-monitoring as a process that occurs during interpersonal interaction. Therefore, these two processes can be encouraged in an articulated way. It is widely recognized in psychology that self-knowledge has a social origin, more particularly in social interactions. It is being built and expanded as the individual observes and describes their behaviors, thoughts, and feelings, the conditions in which they occur, and the consequences they lead to. It also includes information about personal resources (ability to observe and describe, family support, etc.) and personal difficulties (deficits, anxiety, failure to discriminate, etc.).

Why is self-knowledge so important in the perspective of social competence? It can be said that it is the basis for predicting and controlling one's own behaviors and interactions in the social world. When the individual is able to describe and explain their own behaviors in terms of the contingencies associated with them (Skinner, 1974), he/she sets the conditions for predicting and regulating them. And this self-knowledge can make it easier to choose courses of action in a social interaction. Therefore, SST programs should provide the conditions to gradually overcome the shortcomings of self-knowledge (Fig. 2.7).

Fig. 2.7 Self-knowledge and choices

2.2.4 *Ethics and Values of Coexistence*

The concepts of ethics and values of coexistence are complex and necessarily refer to different philosophical and psychological approaches. It is not the purpose here to analyze the theoretical aspects of these terms in depth but rather to interpret them in their narrow sense and relate them to social competence criteria.

In any society, probably without exceptions, individuals are guided by norms and rules about tolerated, approved, or valued behavior patterns of conduct for different situations and interpersonal tasks. One of the oldest prescriptions of conduct, valued until nowadays, is the so-called Golden Rule, already mentioned above (Fig. 2.8).

Notwithstanding differences between groups and subcultures, it is important to recognize values of coexistence in association with the notions of human rights, justice, equity, freedom, dignity, and compassion. These values of coexistence are implicit in the ethical dimension of social competence and, therefore, should be encouraged in SST programs.

Fig. 2.8 Values of coexistence in practice

What Are Values of Coexistence?

As already mentioned, the evaluative character of social competence is not restricted to only one of the sides of interaction and not only to the dyads involved in a certain social task, as it also includes the social group. Assessment applied to a single individual of the interaction limits the construct of social competence to immediate gains and only to this individual, in terms of fulfilling objectives and self-esteem. In this limited sense, coercive, seductive, or deceitful behavior, etc., could be considered socially competent. As already seen, these behaviors cannot be considered as such because they do not meet the ethical dimension of social competence. This limited understanding of social competence, as well as the focus only on social skills, can be found in the contradictory evidence produced by studies on problematic interpersonal relationships.

The criteria of functionality proposed by Linehan (1984) already broadened the focus from the individual to the two participants in the interaction: in addition to achieving immediate goals and maintaining/improving self-esteem, interaction should contribute to maintaining or improving the quality of the relationship, which necessarily includes the two sides of interaction. The other criteria, especially those of the ethical dimension, proposed by the authors reinforce the perspective of the other and of the social group. In the case of bullying, the ethical dimension also implies considering the criteria of balance of power and respect for interpersonal rights in relationships (see A. Del Prette & Del Prette, 2001; Z. Del Prette & Del Prette, 1999).

Therefore, the values of coexistence can be understood as results or consequences of behavioral patterns that combine what is good for the person, for the other, and for the culture (Dittrich & Abib, 2004). Under these conditions, SST programs have been included among the cultural practices consecrated as *cultural goods*, applied to social behavior (Carrara, Silva, & Verdu, 2009).

What Are the Values of Coexistence Pertinent to Social Competence?

This question is difficult to answer, especially in general normative terms, as each social grouping constructs specific values, which guide certain patterns of social behavior. It is understood that, at the beginning of the twenty-first century, there is still much to discuss about values of coexistence, in particular, those related to the ethical dimension of social competence. Even so, the task of identifying values of coexistence assumed in the therapeutic processes in general, and in the SST programs in particular, should be part of the socially relevant professional action.

Fig. 2.9 Balance of power

The principle of the balance of power focuses on the reciprocity value of exchanges, emphasizing the *win-win* premise between people in an interaction. In the perspective presented here, it is understood that this balance is dynamic over time, including temporary and specific delays, but with relatively fair balance, in the medium and long term, of benefits and costs between the interacting parties (Fig. 2.9).

The principle of human rights supposes guarantees in the constitution of a country, normalizing values of dignity, equality, freedom of expression, etc. Any behavior that impairs these institutional guarantees could be subject to legal action. Considering the criteria of social competence, this principle extends and broadens the notion of rights established in the Universal Declaration of Human Rights (of which Brazil is a signatory), to the micro context of interpersonal relations. These are values of coexistence, arising from respect for life, dignity, and free expression, explicitly found in the discourse and ethical norms of most Western societies (Fig. 2.10).

Fig. 2.10 Human rights

Respect and adherence to rights cannot therefore be overlooked or neglected in interpersonal relationships. The following can be mentioned:

- All people are born free and equal in dignity and rights and should act toward one another in a spirit of brotherhood.
- Everyone is entitled to the right to freedom of opinion and expression.
- Everyone has the right to freedom of thought, conscience, and religion; this right includes freedom to change his/her beliefs and manifest them provided that he/she respects the same rights to others.
- Persons of socioeconomic, physical, and/or mental disadvantage, whatever the source of the disadvantage, should be supported by the family and/or the state in order to have the opportunity to enjoy a decent life as much as possible.

To sum up, the two overarching general principles, human rights and balance of power, bring to the context of SST programs the perspective of the interlocutor and the social group, which are not under direct intervention. These principles should firstly guide the therapist's or facilitator's[1] practice and, gradually, relationships

[1] The term facilitator is used to designate someone who conducts a social skills training program (a teacher or other health or education professional).

between the participants and them with other people. It is understood that these two principles cannot be considered separately, neither when preparing SST programs (objectives and procedures) nor in the analysis of their results. In other words, an SST program should not merely produce an *inversion of power* between controllers and those who are controlled, punitive agents and victims, but, as far as possible, maximize the balance of power relationships and fairer exchanges between people. It should also be considered that coercion or harmful relationships, as widely recognized in psychology, are highly likely to lead to counter-control, avoidance, and psychotic reactions. On the other hand, the acquisitions that favor the group also establish a more advantageous context for maintaining and expanding the gains obtained in SST programs.

References

Azzi, R. G. (2011). Desengajamento moral na perspectiva da teoria social cognitiva [Moral disengagement in social cognitive theory]. *Psicologia: Ciência e Profissão, 31*(2), 208–219.

Bandura, A. (1986). *Social foundations of thought and action: A social cognitive theory.* Englewood Cliffs, NJ: Prentice Hall Inc.

Bandura, A. (2008). O exercício da agência humana pela eficácia coletiva [The exercise of human agency through collective efficacy] In: A. Bandura, R. G. Azzi, & S. Polydoro (Orgs.), *Teoria Social Cognitiva: Conceitos básicos [Social cognitive theory: Basic concepts]* (pp. 114–122). Porto Alegre, Brazil: Artmed.

Bolsoni-Silva, A. T., & Carrara, K. (2010). Habilidades sociais e Análise do Comportamento: Compatibilidades e dissensões conceitual-metodológicas [Social skills and behavioral analysis: Compatibilities and conceptual and methodological divergences]. *Psicologia em Revista, 16*(2), 330–350.

Carrara, K., Silva, A. T. B., & Verdu, A. C. M. A. (2009). Metacontingências, THS e estratégias de inclusão: Dimensões e instrumentos compatíveis com o tema transversal da ética? [Meta contingencies, SST and strategies for inclusion: are the dimensions and instruments compatible with ethical principles?] In: R. C. Wielenska. (Org.), *Sobre comportamento e cognição: Desafios, soluções e questionamentos [About Behavior and Cognition: Challenges, Solutions and questions]* (pp. 45–55). Santo André: ESETec.

Comodo, C. N. (2016). Vítimas e autores de bullying: Uma avaliação das habilidades sociais e de indicadores da competência social [Victims, authors and bystanders of bullying: An assessment of social skills and social competence indicators] Doctoral thesis. Graduate Program in Psychology. Federal University of São Carlos.

Del Prette, A. (1982). Treinamento Comportamental junto à população não clínica de baixa renda: Uma análise descritiva de procedimento [Behavioral training with the low-income nonclinical population: A descriptive analysis of the procedure]. Masters dissertation. Psychology Graduate Program. Pontifical Catholic University of Campinas.

Del Prette, A., & Del Prette, Z. A. P. (2001). *Psicologia das relações interpessoais e habilidades sociais: Vivências para o trabalho em grupo [The psychology of interpersonal relationships and social skills: Experiential activities for groups]* (1st ed.). Petrópolis, Brazil: Vozes.

Del Prette, Z. A. P., & Del Prette, A. (1999). *Psicologia das Habilidades Sociais: Terapia, Educação e Trabalho [The psychology of social skills: Therapy, education and work]* (1st ed.). Petrópolis, Brazil: Vozes.

Del Prette, Z. A. P., & Del Prette, A. (2005). *Psicologia das habilidades Sociais na Infância: Teoria e Prática [Psychology of social skills in childhood: Theory and practice]* (1st ed.). Petrópolis, Brazil: Vozes.

Del Prette, Z. A. P., & Del Prette, A. (2010). Habilidades Sociais e Análise do Comportamento: Proximidade histórica e atualidades [Social skills and behavior analysis: Historical connection and new issues]. *Perspectivas em Análise do Comportamento, 1*(2), 104–115.

Dias, T. P., Casali, G. I., Del Prette, A., & Del Prette, Z. A. P. (2019). Automonitoria na competência social: Análise das classes e indicadores comportamentais [Self-monitoring in social competence: Analysis of classes and behavioral indicators). *Acta Comportamentalia, 27*(3), 333–350.

Dittrich, A. (2010). Análise de consequências como procedimento para decisões éticas [Consequence analysis as a procedure in ethical decision making]. *Perspectivas em Análise do Comportamento, 1*(1), 44–54.

Dittrich, A., & Abib, J. A. D. (2004). O sistema ético skinneriano Consequências para a prática dos analistas do comportamento [The Skinnerian ethical system Consequences for behavior analysts' practice]. *Psicologia: Reflexão e Crítica, 17*(3), 427–443.

Dowd, T., & Tierney, J. (2005). *Teaching social skills to youth: A step-by-step guide to 182 basic to complex skills plus helpful teaching techniques*. Crawford, Nebraska: Boys Town Press.

Glenn, S. (2005). Metacontingências em Walden Dois [Meta contingencies in Walden two]. In J. C. Todorov, R. C. Martone, & M. G. Borges (Eds.), *Metacongingências, comportamento, cultura e sociedade [Metacontingencies, Behavior, Culture and Society]* (pp. 13–28). Santo Andre (SP), Brazil: ESETec Editores Associados.

Gresham, F. M. (2009). Análise do comportamento aplicada às habilidades sociais [Analysis of behavior applied to social skills] In: A. Del Prette, & Z. A. P. Del Prette (Orgs.), *Psicologia das habilidades sociais: Diversidade teórica e suas implicações [The Psychology of Social Skills: Theoretical Diversity and its Implications]* (pp. 17–66). Petrópolis, Brazil: Vozes.

Hunziker, M. L., & Moreno, R. (2000). Análise da noção de variabilidade Comportamental [Analysis of the of behavioral variability concept]. *Psicologia: Teoria e Pesquisa, 16*(2), 135–145.

Linehan, M. M. (1984). Interpersonal effectiveness in assertive situations. In E. E. Bleechman (Ed.), *Behavior modification with women*. New York: Guilford Press.

McFall, R. M. (1982). A review and reformulation of the concept of social skills. *Behavioral Assessment, 4*, 1–33.

Mischel, W. (1958). Preference for delayed reinforcement: An experimental study of a cultural observation. *The Journal of Abnormal and Social Psychology, 56*, 57–61.

Olaz, F. O., Medrano, L. A. & Cabanillas, G. A. (2017). Programa vivencial versus programa instrucional de habilidades sociais: impacto sobre a autoeficácia de universitários [Experiential program versus instructional social skills program: impact on university students´ self-efficacy]. In A. Del Prette, & Z. A. P. Prette, (Orgs.), *Habilidades sociais: Intervenções efetivas em grupo [Social skills: Effective group interventions]* (3ird. ed.) (pp. 175–202). São Paulo, Brazil: Casa do Psicólogo.

Polydoro, S. & Azzi, R. G. (2008). Autorregulação: Aspectos introdutórios [Self-regulation: Introductory aspects]. In: A. Bandura, R. G. Azzi, & S. Polydoro (Orgs.), *Teoria Social Cognitiva: Conceitos básicos [Social cognitive theory: Basic concepts]* (pp. 149–164). Porto Alegre, Brazil: Artmed.

Rachlin, H. (1974). Self-control. *Behavior, 2*, 94–107.

Rangel, P. C. N. (2010). *Variabilidade Comportamental: Uma comparação entre pessoas jovens e idosas [Behavioral Variability: A comparison between young and old people]*. Doctoral thesis. Institute of Psychology, University de Brasilia. Brasília (DF), Brazil.

Schlundt, D. G., & McFall, R. M. (1985). New directions in the assessment of social competence and social skills. In L. L' Abate & M. A. Milan (Eds.), *Handbook of social skills training and research* (pp. 22–49). New York: Wiley.

Skinner, B. F. (1968). *The Technology of Teaching*. New York: Appleton-Century-Crofts.

Skinner, B. F. (1974). *About Behaviorism*. New York: Knopf.

Chapter 3
Interpersonal Tasks and Cultural Practices

Abstract We address the notions of interpersonal tasks, social roles, and cultural practices as contexts relevant to understanding social skills, social competence, and also client deficits and resources to deal with interpersonal demands. The aim of this discussion is to highlight the possible contribution of social competence to outline new cultural practices in different sectors of human coexistence.

Keywords Social competence · Interpersonal task · Cultural practices

Social skills and competence are not intrinsic traits of an individual, but rather they are related to classes and subclasses of social skills and to interpersonal behavior assessment, according to a set of criteria. Assessment is done by observing and/or describing behaviors and for this purpose considers the characteristics of the immediate environment, situation, and culture. Social behavior must be contextualized, therefore, in order to obtain a more pertinent description and more accurate assessment. This contextualization refers to other important and related concepts, emphasizing those of social tasks, social roles, and cultural practices. On the other hand, the contextualization of behavior in interactive tasks and social roles is indispensable to identifying relevant deficits that should direct intervention programs.

3.1 The Concept of Interpersonal Tasks

According to McFall (1982), a social task is an identifiable segment of interaction within a culture, in response to the question about people interacting: *what are they doing?* Every social interaction can, therefore, be understood as a sequence of behavioral exchanges, where those involved fulfil one or more social tasks.

The concept of interpersonal tasks adopted in this book is very similar to McFall's (1982) of social tasks. However, substituting the term social for interpersonal is justified given that social competence assessment concerns not only the behavior of one of the interlocutors but of the two or more people interacting.

Z. A. P. Del Prette, A. Del Prette, *Social Competence and Social Skills*,
https://doi.org/10.1007/978-3-030-70127-7_3

The notion of interpersonal tasks makes it easier to identify demands present during the interaction, thus facilitating the description of a person's behavior (if comprised or not of social skills) and its results (whether they achieve social competence or not). McFall (1982) asserts that social tasks[1] can be hierarchically organized, so that a more complex task can be decomposed into smaller tasks. For example, the task of *finding a romantic partner* can be subdivided into smaller units, such as *make initial contact, set dates, encourage the other's interest, increase intimacy,* etc. In the opposite sense of composition of an activity, when, for example, a therapist asks their client how an interaction with their child went, this question is part of the professional interpersonal task of the therapist *to probe* within a therapeutic context. And this probing may be a component of interpersonal clinical care tasks (Fig. 3.1).

Fig. 3.1 Finding a romantic partner

Every person encounters a variety of interpersonal tasks in their day-to-day life. Each one can require different classes of social skills and different combinations of these classes. The concept of interpersonal tasks is, therefore, related to social skills, but they do not overlap. An interpersonal task is an interactive sequence between people, identifiable in a situation and culture in terms of beginning, middle, and end. The concept of social skills is descriptive of each individual's behavior applied to the behaviors that can be classified as such, as defined in Chap. 1.

The concept of interpersonal tasks is indispensable for analyzing and identifying client's deficits and resources in social skills and other requisites of social competence. The relevant deficits and resources depend on the relevant interpersonal tasks of the client's daily life associated with the roles that they take on and whose exercise may require specific social skills, as shown below.

3.2 Social Skills and Social Roles

The social skills described in the Portfolio (Chap. 1) can also be reorganized according to the social roles people take on over their lifetimes. Social roles are culturally determined and involve behavioral patterns expected by the social group (or self-attributed) while exercising certain functions in specific contexts and activities. Some social roles are complementary (e.g., husband-wife, parents-children, teacher-student) and, therefore, refer to relationship patterns between the pairs involved.

Socially competent behaviors associated to certain social roles can be essential to the satisfaction and well-being of those involved in the interpersonal tasks. Difficulties or attempts to improve these roles generally implies in identifying

[1] Hereinafter referred to as interpersonal tasks, as explained.

classes and subclasses of social skills that characterize them or that may better qualify them. In most societies, both in intercountry relations and in group-individual interactions, interpersonal tasks are arbitrated in this perspective. Considering the conceptual and empirical research and developments already carried out in our country,[2] a set of social skills (SS) pertinent to various roles can be listed (Table 3.1):

Table 3.1 Social skills associated with specific social roles

Social role	Set of social skills
Couples SS	Expressing positive feelings and empathy (understanding, feelings, desires, positive opinions, praising, and thanking); being assertive (stating preferences, feelings and opinions, defending the right for respect to one's own individuality, making requests and reinforcing the fulfilment of agreements, asking for clarification, disagreeing, requesting changes in behavior); maintaining self-control during potentially stressful situations (such as when receiving criticism from or being the object of a partner's teasing, when in an emotionally altered state, or when facing various problems); recognizing a partner's emotional changes or difficulties; calming oneself and one's partner
Educational SS (parents)	Expressing affection toward children, observing and identifying children's feelings and behaviors, having conversations, presenting and/or suggesting activities, establishing and providing consequences, putting forward problems and games, encouraging, providing guidance with school work, encouraging reading and reflecting, evaluating/questioning behavior, mediating children's interaction with other people, encouraging feedback and being kind to others, discussing values, criteria, and social norms, encouraging children's autonomy, reciprocity, and empathy
Pedagogical SS (teachers)	Planning, structuring, and presenting interactive activities (setting objectives and goals for activities, selecting and providing materials, showing content); conducting interactive activities (showing, explaining, and evaluating through dialogue); assessing activities and specific behaviors (asking for and giving feedback individually and to the class, approving, complimenting behaviors, correcting without punishing, disagreeing, correcting constructively); cultivating affection and student participation (demonstrating support, good humor, meeting requests for private conversations, encouraging and mediating others' participation (such as parents)) in activities with the students
Academic SS (students)	Paying attention to the teacher when they speak; asking and answering questions; listening to a classmate's opinion; expressing opinions; asking for help from teachers or classmates; fulfilling classmates' requests; coordinating study groups; giving suggestions about classroom topics; borrowing/lending materials; organizing/participating in extracurricular activities (sports, visits to museums, theatres, etc.)
Professional SS	They involve many of the previous behaviors but also some more specific ones such as laying out plans and organizational policies, organizing and conducting meetings, suggesting projects, assigning and asking for tasks, conducting interviews, organizing and presenting results, listening to suggestions, dealing with complaints, giving guidance to colleagues and staff, trying to solve problems, establishing and communicating rules, accepting/denying requests
Caregivers SS (elderly and sick)	This involves many of the educational social skills already mentioned but also others, such as handling socially inappropriate or self-harming behaviors, resistance to medication, self-control of stress, emotional support, etc.

[2] Those who are interested can find publications about each of these items in search engines, and especially at www.rihs.ufscar.br.

This list does not exhaust the possibilities of social roles that require specific social skills. A social skills repertoire can be evaluated in greater or less detail, depending on the focus of the client's complaint and the objectives of the intervention. For example, studies on professional social skills may even require subdivisions of professional functions, such as directors, managers, and employees of different core activities.

Considering the social roles and respective social skills required in them, contextualized in specific interpersonal tasks, a more pertinent analysis of the possible deficits and resources of the client can be made. Moreover, this analysis is indispensable for establishing socially relevant intervention objectives.

3.3 Social Skills Deficits

From an early age, families make an effort to teach their children to interact with others. With each interpersonal task they are faced with, people also learn and improve, especially through instructions, models, and consequences, new social skills and social competence requirements. However, when the environment is not favorable, there may be deficits in these requirements and concurrent behaviors, which usually result in interpersonal difficulties, requiring professional care.

A social skills portfolio can help put classes into subclasses of social skills and is especially important for Social Skills Training (SST) programs as it makes it easier to identify the client's resources (what they already have), as well as their deficits or difficulties in certain social skills and other social competence requisites.

In a more refined analysis, identifying the types of social skills deficits can help select more appropriate procedures for the intervention. Thus, three types of social skills deficits can be characterized (Gresham, 2009; Del Prette & Del Prette, 2005) with reference to the indicated procedures to overcome them.

Acquisition Deficits These take place when a skill does not exist in the repertoire and must be learned, thus requiring teaching procedures (modeling, behavioral rehearsal, and arranging the environment for them to be valued in the environment).

Performance Deficit This happens when the skill is present in a client's repertoire but is not used very often or without adequate discrimination of a situation, interlocutor, or occasions that demand the skill. This case requires discrimination training for demands and rearranging motivational factors so that the client's attempts obtain positive consequences.

Fluency Deficit This is characterized by flaws in topography and by high response cost for the behavior, which affect its effectiveness, requiring procedures such as feedback, modelling, and instruction for enhancing the skill.

3.4 Social Competence and Cultural Practices

Each person is born in a given cultural context, with varied cultural practices from caring for children, to eating, to producing resources, to having fun, etc. Cultural practices involve a variety of tasks, many of which are interpersonal tasks pertinent to the different, and generally complimentary, social roles assumed by individuals. These tasks also require specific skills associated to these different roles. In other words, the same person may be involved in interpersonal tasks linked to overlapping roles, which require social skills that are not always superimposed, for example, parental, educational, and marital.

Cultural practices are transmitted to members and reproduced from generation to generation until they are substituted by others when they cease to be functional to that culture or to groups with greater power that benefit from them. Thus, some practices, even if they are not beneficial, are maintained for many generations. An example of this is provided by Glenn (2005), when differentiating cultural and technological processes (based on contingencies that produce desirable outcomes for the group, favorable to survival and quality of life) from ceremonial processes (maintained by those who detain power and authority, regardless of another's outcome).

Notwithstanding the possible negative connotation associated with the term *technological*, which is being called technological cultural processes, known as utopians for most societies today, is coherent with the ethical dimension of social competence when considering SST programs, guided by this construct, conducted in collective contexts such as family, school, specific sectors of organizations, etc. It is ultimately about promoting individual behaviors and interpersonal relationships that benefit not only the individual but also the group, recognizing the necessary collective interdependence as the basis for well-being, social peace, and quality of life.

The influence of culture over social skills and social competence is already implicit in the definition of both these concepts. However, it is also possible to conceive that when changes in patterns of coexistence, within smaller social niches (family, work, and educational relationships, among others), attain visibility regarding their instrumental and ethical impact, they could, under certain circumstances, be generalized and eventually lead to changes in cultural practices.

It is understood that the ethical and instrumental dimensions inherent to social competence criteria effectively point toward new patterns of interpersonal relations (Del Prette & Del Prette, 2001). However, it is also recognized that it is not yet possible to gauge the scope and effects of the contribution of the field of social skills to culture, since interventions are still reasonably restricted, lacking dissemination and universal preventive programs (Dowd & Tierney, 2005; Elliott & Gresham, 2007). Nevertheless, evidence of the effectiveness of social skills programs in schools on reducing aggression and conflict and promoting more harmonious relationships (Goldstein, Sprafkin, Gershaw, & Klein, 1980) has generated proposals for broader social-emotional development projects already implemented in other countries and, more recently, beginning to be also used in Brazil.

The potential of social skill training oriented to ethical patterns has begun to be recognized by various scholars and researchers. Carrara, Silva, and Verdu (2006, 2009) place social skills programs among practices compatible with an ethical perspective applied to social behavior and beneficial to culture.

References

Carrara, K., Silva, A. T. B., & Verdu, A. C. M. A. (2006). Delineamentos culturais e práticas descritas por políticas públicas: Análise conceitual e projetos de intervenção [Cultural designs and practices described by public policies: Conceptual analysis and intervention projects]. In: H. H. Guillhardi, & N. C. de Aguirre (Orgs.), *Sobre comportamento e cognição: Expondo a variabilidade [About Behavior and Cognition: Exposing the variability]* (pp. 354-366). Santo André: ESETec.

Carrara, K., Silva, A. T. B., & Verdu, A. C. M. A. (2009). Metacontingências, THS e estratégias de inclusão: Dimensões e instrumentos compatíveis com o tema transversal da ética? [Meta contingencies, SST and strategies for inclusion: are the dimensions and instruments compatible with ethical principles?] In: R. C. Wielenska. (Org.), *Sobre comportamento e cognição: Desafios, soluções e questionamentos [About Behavior and Cognition: Challenges, solutions and questions]* (pp. 45–55). Santo André: ESETec.

Del Prette, A. & Del Prette, Z. A. P. (2001). *Psicologia das relações interpessoais e habilidades sociais: Vivências para o trabalho em grupo [The psychology of interpersonal relationships and social skills: Experiential activities for groups]* (1st.ed.). Petrópolis, Brazil: Vozes.

Del Prette, Z. A. P., & Del Prette, A. (2005). Psicologia das habilidades Sociais na Infância: Teoria e Prática [Psychology of social skills in childhood: Theory and practice] (1st.ed.). Petrópolis, Brazil: Vozes.

Dowd, T., & Tierney, J. (2005). *Teaching social skills to youth: A step-by-step guide to 182 basic to complex skills plus helpful teaching techniques*. Crawford, Nebraska: Boys Town Press.

Elliott, S. M., & Gresham, F. M. (2007). *Classwide intervention program teacher's guide*. Minneapolis, MN: NCS Pearson.

Glenn, S. (2005). Metacontingências em Walden Dois [Meta contingencies in Walden Two] In: J. C. Todorov, R. C. Martone & M. G. Borges (2005). *Metacongingências, comportamento, cultura e sociedade [Metacontingencies, Behavior, Culture and Society]* (pp. 13–28). Santo Andre/SP: ESETec Editores Associados.

Goldstein, A. P., Sprafkin, R. P., Gershaw, N. J. Klein, P. (1980). *Skillstreaming the adolescent: A structured approach to teaching prosocial skills*. Champaign, IL: Research Press Company.

Gresham, F. M. (2009). Análise do comportamento aplicada às habilidades sociais [Analysis of behavior applied to social skills]. In: A. Del Prette, & Z. A. P. Del Prette (Orgs.), *Psicologia das habilidades sociais: Diversidade teórica e suas implicações [The Psychology of Social Skills: Theoretical Diversity and its Implications]* (pp. 17–66). Petrópolis: Vozes.

McFall, R. M. (1982). A review and reformulation of the concept of social skills. *Behavioral Assessment, 4*, 1–33.

Chapter 4
Programs and the Experiential Method

Abstract In this chapter, we present the rationale for Social Skills Training (SST) programs based on the positive correlations and problems associated with social skills deficits and other requirements of social competence. Regarding these considerations, a brief presentation is made on preventive, therapeutic, and professional programs, as well as on the possibilities of interventions in group and individual formats. At the end of this chapter, we present the rationale of the experiential method, defining experiential activities and their use for promoting social skills and social competence.

Keywords Social Skills Training · Experiential method · Preventive intervention · Therapeutic intervention

In addition to its potential importance in shaping new cultural practices, the need to promote social skills and social competence, whether through parent and school education procedures or through SST programs (therapeutic, preventive, and professional), can be justified by two strands, drawn from research in the area. The first addresses the positive correlates associated to a good social skills repertoire. The second refers to the correlation between social skill deficits and various psychological disorders or problems together with the positive outcomes of these programs. These two strands are presented in following.

4.1 Positive Correlations of Good Social Skills Repertoires

Research in the field of social skills has accumulated evidence of positive and desired outcomes associated to good social skill repertoires, some highlighting the protective role that repertoire has in avoiding psychological disorders and development problems. Table 4.1 summarizes the main positive elements commonly identified in studies in the field.

Z. A. P. Del Prette, A. Del Prette, *Social Competence and Social Skills*,
https://doi.org/10.1007/978-3-030-70127-7_4

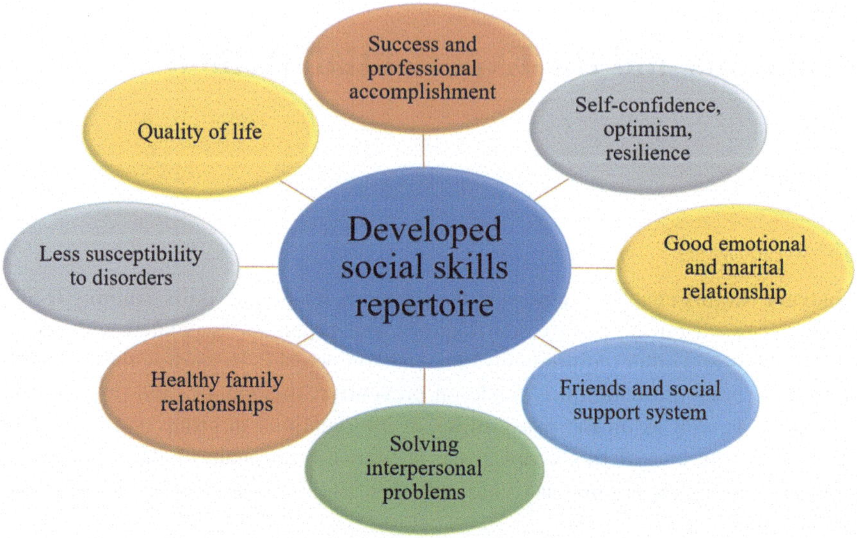

Fig. 4.1 Positive correlations of a developed social skills repertoire

Figure 4.1 shows that a good repertoire in social skills and social competence is related to various indicators of well-being, which are coherent with the current, wider, concept of health (Brasil, 2010), particularly mental health. According to this concept, the assessment of well-being is an important indicator to be considered (Abreu, Barletta, & Murta, 2015) and goes beyond factors such as eating, housing, access to schools, and safety. It should also include the quality of social coexistence and its correlations, as shown in Fig. 4.1. It is therefore justified to invest in the promotion of social skills and social competence of the population in general, since it supports other health promotion strategies, as advocated in government policies in many countries, especially concerning children, adolescence, and old age.

4.2 Problems Associated with Social Skills Deficits

Social skills deficits are associated, in general, to specific psychological problems and disorders, such as depression, anxiety, social isolation, problematic behaviors, learning difficulties, consumption of psychoactive drugs, etc. (Caballo, 2003; Del Prette & Del Prette, 2001, 2017). For this reason, social skills deficits are recognized as risk factors for psychosocial functioning.

Del Prette, Falcone, and Murta (2013) observed that concerning personality disorders, the symptoms listed in the *Diagnostic and Statistical Manual of Mental Disorders* (DSM-IV, APA, 2000) include direct and indirect references to social skills deficit patterns. Summarizing the results found in this analysis, they identified that (a) for disorders in Cluster A (*schizotypal*, *schizoid*, and *paranoid personality disorders*), the skills most predominantly found deficient were those for controlling anger and aggressiveness (only for paranoid personalities), expressing empathy, holding conversations, expressing positive affect, and being expressive in general; (b) for disorders belonging to Cluster B (antisocial, borderline, histrionic, and narcissistic personalities), interpersonal patterns do not typically meet the ethical criteria of social competence (valuing and respecting others), as well as evidence of the lack of authentic emotiveness and deficits in assertive and empathic social skills; (c) for disorders in Cluster C (dependent, avoidant, and obsessive-compulsive personalities), deficits in assertiveness prevail, and each one of these disorders is also associated to more diverse social skills deficits, including empathy, problem-solving, and emotional expressiveness.

Behavioral problems, which compete with social skills, are associated with social skills deficits. Behaviors such as mutism, alienation, aggressive demands, and refusing food are intermittently brought about by advice, exhortations, and even warnings and punishment. These procedures mostly work by strengthening such behaviors.

4.3 Social Skills Training (SST) Programs

Any intervention program, whether it is therapeutic or educational, can be defined as an arrangement of structured conditions in order to achieve certain previously established objectives. This description connects two indispensable components of any program: conditions and objectives. The conditions refer to a set of techniques, procedures, and resources available for use; the objectives are the desired and expected results obtained by the end of the program. These two components are also at the base of the definition for Social Skills Training (SST) programs oriented toward social competence (Fig. 4.2).

The relevance of the objectives of an SST program ultimately depends on the impact they might have on the client's interpersonal relations and quality of life. An

> **Social Skills Program oriented to Social Competence** is a set of planned activities used to structure learning processes, mediated, and led by a therapist or facilitator, aiming not only at acquiring and/or perfecting Social Skills, but also the other requirements for Social Competence.

Fig. 4.2 Programs oriented to social competence

SST program oriented toward social competence should go beyond the four first objectives listed below (usually mentioned in the literature) and include all of the following:

- Increasing the frequency and proficiency of those social skills already learned but still deficient
- Learning new and significant social skills
- Eliminating or reducing behaviors that compete with those social skills
- Refining discrimination of interpersonal tasks that may be present in the social environment
- Increasing the variability of social skills
- Developing values of coexistence, following the perspective of respect for human rights, in interactions with others
- Improving self-monitoring and self-knowledge, associated to social behavior

4.4 SST Program Applications and Clientele

Social skill deficits arise when learning processes do not occur naturally or occur for concurrent problematic behavior, and overcoming these deficits almost always requires specialized care. This is usually done through structured learning conditions called programs.

SST programs may be conducted in group or individual format. They can be of a preventative, therapeutic, or professional nature and be used with a wide range of age groups. In the educational context, preventative SST programs stand out, targeted at children and adolescents aiming to reduce problems such as lack of discipline, aggressiveness, bullying, prejudice, drug addiction, etc. In the clinical context, therapeutic SST programs, in groups or individually, are used for different problems across all age groups. In a professional situation, SST programs are recommended for addressing a variety of issues from preparing young people for the transition to the job market to improving, later on, the interpersonal conditions related to productivity, to searching for new opportunities and health during retirement.

Social skills programs have been widely used in school contexts for fostering socioemotional development and preventing behavioral problems, in which both have been demonstrated to give support for academic performance and to act as a mechanism for the inclusion of children with sensory, motor, and mental deficiencies. In this context, generally with parents' and teachers' participation, SST programs can be used at three levels (Gresham, 2009), related to different degrees of psychosocial attention:

Universal: programs catering for all the children in a classroom or the whole school, regardless of identified problems or risk factors

Selective: programs for small groups in a vulnerable situation or that would not benefit from universal programs

Indicated: programs for children with problems, in an individual format such as therapy, preceded by a detailed functional assessment of the complaint and other associated disturbances

This same scheme can be used for other population strata, such as young people in conflict with the law, elderly people in special communities, women victims of abuse, etc. The programs described are of a therapeutic nature and have as a base the multimodal and functional assessment which requires more time, necessarily including participation from parents and other significant ones.

The SST programs for psychological problems or disorders can be planned and conducted (a) as the main intervention of therapeutic care and (b) as a complementary intervention to therapy for which SST is recommended. Table 4.1 lists the main problems and disorders for each cluster and for which SST is most recommended.

Table 4.1 Psychological problems and disorders for which SST is indicated as primary or complementary intervention

Main intervention	Complementary intervention
✓ Shyness/social isolation	✓ Learning difficulties
✓ Social anxiety	✓ ADHD and behavioral problems
✓ Social phobia	✓ Schizophrenia and psychotic spectrum
✓ Aggressiveness	✓ STDs and AIDS
✓ Delinquency	✓ ASD (autism)
✓ Unipolar depression	✓ Sensory, mental, and physical deficiencies
✓ Marital problems	✓ Chemical dependency
✓ Family problems	✓ Persistent depressive disorder

The problems and disorders for which SST is recommended for use as the main intervention strategy are those which present the most impairment in interpersonal relations, associated with social skill deficits and/or concurrent behavior. Such problems are referred to different professionals in the area of health, such as psychotherapists, psychiatrists, psycho-educationalists, etc.

An analysis of the two groups of *SST application* highlights the scope of this type of intervention and the importance of training the psychologist and other health and education professionals in this area.

The problems and disorders for which SST is suggested as a complementary tool for intervention are those in which social skills deficits are one of the factors involved and should therefore be included in a multimodal intervention. In most of these disorders, there are no sufficient conclusive data available about the role social skills play (if they are the cause or consequence of the disorder). There is, however, evidence (Del Prette, Del Prette, Gresham, & Vance, 2012; Monti, Kadden, Rohsenow, Cooney, & Abrams, 2005) that a good social skills repertoire acts as a protective factor for healthy development, mental health, and for a more favorable response to treatment. It is understood that professional training in this area should include training in at least the following items:

- Understanding the conceptual bases of the social skills field
- Using resources, techniques, and assessment procedures in the area
- Experience in conducting SST groups and/or individual SST programs, using therapeutic resources, techniques, and procedures for intervention
- Using instruments and materials necessary for assessing and interpreting the results obtained

Given the breadth of possibilities for using SST programs, this training should be part of the undergraduate curriculum in psychology and similar areas. Unfortunately, programs that take this into account are still rare.

4.4.1 Social Skills Programs in Individual Intervention

Social Skills Training has been widely used in the context of individual intervention (see, e.g., Hagar, Goldstein, & Brooks, 2006). The conceptual base, objectives, and techniques for group SST are equally applicable to individual treatment. The program can be a complement to therapeutic care or may be the main component used during treatment. In both cases, some adaptations to the usual strategies and procedures in group programs may be necessary (Fig. 4.3).

Fig. 4.3 SST in individual intervention

Concerning adults, adolescents, and children, the SST program is planned from the initial assessment of deficits, concurrent behaviors, and resources identified by the therapist in conjunction with the main complaint. Regarding children, it is usually defined in answer to parents' requests, who express specific complaints in this area, based on their own observations, or those of teachers and other significant ones. In many cases, parents arrive with a diagnosis of their own such as *relationship problems*, *shyness*, or *aggressiveness*, and most of the time they are correct but have difficulty in accepting that they are also part of the problem.

4.5 The Experiential Method

Procedures, resources, and techniques commonly used in SST programs can be identified by analyzing the classic manuals (e.g., Curran & Monti, 1982; Dowd & Tierney, 2005; Elliott & Gresham, 2007; Greene & Burleson, 2003; Hargie, Saunders, & Dickson, 1994). They were mostly developed according to behavioral, cognitive, and cognitive-behavioral approaches.

A wide range of SST programs can be observed, each with different technical proposals, with greater or lesser emphasis on instructional procedures and focused on bigger or smaller units of social skills. Nevertheless, the key to the effectiveness of any program is to establish conditions which allow the behavior to occur and to alter it in the expected and desired direction. An alternative that has been developed over the last decades, with evidence of its effectiveness, has been the use of experiential activities for promoting social skills alongside the other requisites for social competence.

Using experiential activities as a base for SST programs is called the experiential method. The effectiveness of this method can be observed in various studies (Braz & Del Prette, 2017; A. Prette & Del Prette, 2003, 2017; Z. Del Prette & Del Prette, 2010; Del Prette, Del Prette, & Barreto, 1999; Del Prette, Rocha, & Del Prette, 2017; Kestenberg & Falcone, 2017; Lopes, 2013; Lopes & Del Prette, 2017; Olaz, Medrano, & Cabanillas, 2017; Pereira, 2010; Pereira-Guizzo & Del Prette, 2017; Rocha, 2009; Vila & Del Prette, 2009).

The experiential method refers to organizing a learning environment in which the therapist obtains direct access to the participant's behavior and helps them acquire new social skills under the perspective of social competence. Thus, the therapist and client can establish objectives together that go beyond reducing concurrent behaviors and learning various social skills, in such a way as to also contemplate the analysis of favorable consequences for both participants of a dyad or all the members of a group and other requirements for social competence.

> The *experiential method* can be defined as the structuring of a practical learning environment that allows not only the use of techniques and procedures common to most SST programs but also establishes additional favorable conditions for promoting social competence.

A brief discussion about experiential activities, the experiential method, and their use for promoting the requisites for social competence can be found next, followed by other techniques, strategies, and resources associated to this method.

4.5.1 What Is an Experiential Activity?

The term experiential activity has been used in psychology for some time now, almost always associated with practice, in workshops, or in human resource training. Having the meaning of something lived through, the use of the term experiential activity goes back to philosophy, more specifically to Dilthey (Amaral, 2004). According to this philosopher, an experiential activity is related to a complete experience of reality and not a fragmented one to the extent that the activity and reality might be confused. It is situated at a midway point between the general and the individual, the universal and the singular, and what is ideal and what is real.

In the initial formulation of the concept of an experiential activity (A. Del Prette & Del Prette, 2001), in the SST programs, categories similar to Dilthey's shaped the main links of the definition of the term. Also, like Dilthey, the term experiential activity was understood as something lived and that can continue to be experienced, in a kind of flashback not only cognitive but mainly behavioral. In other words, what was *experienced* by the participant, that is, an experiential return of the situation lived.

However, in the meaning used by Del Prette and Del Prette (2001), an experiential activity does not refer exclusively to a past experience but also to something that may still occur. Thus, it may be a new experience that can happen because it resides in the predictable order of every daily life. In both, the participants experience interpersonal tasks specific to structured situations in the context of the session.

Fig. 4.4 Analogous experiential activity

An experiential activity is a time to experience the general/universal, the singular, and the ideal. The general/universal is reflected in the behavioral rules that show contingencies established by culture (or cultures): *when* you do it and *if* you do so. The singular refers exclusively to the experience of each one, which is unique but possible of different interpretations. The ideal refers to behaviors (observed in yourself and in others) that are goals of a client or a group of participants. It may be the objective or target behavior that the client seeks to learn or develop, in compatibility with the group subculture and also with the therapist's assessment. Considering the activities that are called experiential, in SST programs, this term is defined as (Fig. 4.4):

An *experiential activity* is ① a structured activity [..]. that ② mobilizes the participants' feelings, thoughts and public behaviors and ③ allows the therapist or facilitator to adopt specific procedures to achieve the program's objectives. (A. Del Prette & Del Prette, 2001, p.106)

4.5.2 Analogous and Symbolic Experiential Activities

According to the activities developed by the therapist, the experiential activities in SST programs can be roughly categorized into two modalities: analogous and symbolic. This classification is related to the different functions of experiential activities in an SST program.

In the analogous experiential activities, the therapist organizes the activity using elements from the client's reality, for example, a boardroom with chairs, table, known (work colleagues) and unknown interlocutors (clients), etc. Moreover, the initial situation can change to create new demands by evaluating and training the participant(s). For example, in a job interview task, you can simulate a phone call to the interviewer and/or the interviewer's boss coming into the situation, etc.

Analogous experiential activities simulate everyday situations already experienced or possible to be experienced by the participants.

Symbolic experiential activities can include allegories, fables, and games. Some of them, presented in this manual, are symbolic, such as the Silence Game (see Chap. 9). Their playful nature can reduce anxiety, thus easing the process of learning new social behaviors, required in day-to-day interactions.

Symbolic experiential activities simulate situations and tasks, generally in a playful manner that do not have a direct correspondent in everyday life but that establish demands for social skills relevant to social life.

Fig. 4.5 Symbolic experiential activity

By using the experiential method, the therapist creates conditions for the client's active participation. An experiential activity favors the observation that behavior has an effect on the environment and that the results of the interactions depend on the individual, the dyad, and the group. This exposure increases the participants' sensitivity to contingencies reasonably similar to those that occur in their natural environment (Fig. 4.5).

The programs that adopt the experiential method to promote social skills and the other requisites for social competence have many advantages, but they depend especially on the therapist's observation and attention in order to be effective. Among the advantages this method offers is that it makes it simpler for the therapist to access the participants' behavior in the *here and now* of the session, whether in individual or group SST programs. This access allows the therapist to:

- Observe a participant's behavior in interpersonal tasks during sessions, identifying resources and difficulties
- Provide consequences and offer prompts for smaller units of behavior
- Use one participant (to act) as a model for the other's behavior
- Provide feedback to the participants and, in the case of group sessions, mediate feedback from participants targeted at the colleague in focus during that activity
- Identify and analyze three-term contingencies (antecedents, behavior, and consequences) with the participants
- Alter the characteristics of an experiential activity, while it plays out, creating new demands for behavior or making those already in place easier

Fig. 4.6 Experiential and Observer Groups

As a rule, the therapist must consider that experiential activities, especially analogous ones, are not just scripts but general instructions for interactive contexts, whose speech must be elaborated by the client, within the possibilities of his behavior repertoire. Except when a particular instruction is given, the participant in training organizes his/her own behavior in the interaction scenario. The activity can involve all the participants, or they can be subdivided into two groups: those that are being trained directly (Experiential Group, or EG) and those that are being trained indirectly (Observer Group, or OG), sometimes with whispered instructions on who to watch and what behaviors to watch out for. In these attributions, the therapist or facilitator must ensure the involvement and cooperation of certain participants and provide, throughout the sessions, a distributed attention in the most equitable way possible for all. Depending on the need, the therapist can change the composition of the groups by switching one or another member of the GO to the GV or vice versa (Fig. 4.6).

Therefore, everyone is being trained simultaneously during an experiential activity. The EG participants learn by directly performing new social skills or improving already learned ones. The other participants, in the OG, learn by observation and also hone their skills of describing, evaluating, and providing feedback about the observed behaviors.

It is important to note that a program is not merely a sequence of experiential activities or themes. The experiential activities should be chosen and used according to the needs and objectives established for the group and for each session. This is done by comparing the objectives of the program, inferred from the participants' portfolio, with those defined in the experiential activities, and then selecting the experiential activities that structure the context favorable to achieving these objectives.

Some experiential activities, symbolic and analogous, which have been tested in group SST programs can be found in Chap. 10 of this manual, as well as other texts (Del Prette & Del Prette, 2001, 2005). Each of them is described in detail in terms of objectives, materials, procedures, observations, and variations.

References

Abreu, S., Barletta, J. B., & Murta, S. G. (2015). Prevenção e promoção em Saúde Mental no curso da vida: Indicadores para a ação [Preventing and promoting mental health over a lifetime: Indicators for action]. In: S. G. Murta, C. Leandro-França, K. Brito dos Santos, & L. Polejack (Orgs.), *Prevenção e promoção em Saúde Mental* (pp. 75–92). Novo Hamburgo, Brazil: Sinopsys.

Amaral, M. N. C. P. (2004). Dilthey: Conceito de vivência e os limites da compreensão nas ciências do espírito [Dilthey: Concept of experience and the limits of the understanding in the sciences of the spirit]. *Trans/Form/Ação: Revista de Filosofia da UNESP, 27*(2), 51–73.

American Psychiatric Association (2000). *Diagnostic and statistical manual of mental disorders* (4th ed., rev.) Washington, DC: Author.

Brasil, Ministério da Saúde, Secretaria de Vigilância em Saúde. (2010) *Política Nacional de Promoção de Saúde*, 3°. Ed. [*National Policy for the Promotion of Health*, 3rd ed]. Brasília, Brazil: Ministério da Saúde.

Braz, A. C., & Del Prette, Z. A. P. (2017). Programa de habilidades sociais assertivas para idosos [Assertive social skills training for the elderly]. In: A. Del Prette, & Z. A. P. Prette, (Orgs.). *Habilidades sociais: Intervenções efetivas em grupo [Social Skills: Effective group interventions]* (3ird. ed.) (pp. 231–260). São Paulo, Brazil: Casa do Psicólogo.

Caballo, V. E. (2003). *Manual de avaliação e treinamento das habilidades sociais [Social skills training and assessment manual]*. São Paulo, Brazil, Santos.

Curran, J. P., & Monti, P. M. (1982). *Social skills training: A practical handbook for assessment and treatment*. New York: The Guilford Press.
Del Prette, A., & Del Prette, Z. A. P. (Orgs), (2017). *Habilidades Sociais: Intervenções efetivas em grupo [Social Skills: Effective group interventions]* (3ird. ed.). São Paulo, Brazil: Casa do Psicólogo.
Del Prette, A. & Del Prette, Z. A. P. (2001). *Psicologia das relações interpessoais e habilidades sociais: Vivências para o trabalho em grupo [The psychology of interpersonal relationships and social skills: Experiential activities for groups]* (1st. ed.). Petrópolis, Brazil: Vozes.
Del Prette, A., & Del Prette, Z. A. P. (2003). No contexto da travessia para o ambiente de trabalho: Treinamento de habilidades sociais com universitários [On the crossing for the work context: Social skills training with undergraduate students]. *Estudos de Psicologia, 8*(3), 413–420.
Del Prette, A., Del Prette, Z. A. P., & Barreto, M. C. M. (1999). Habilidades sociales en la formación del psicólogo: Análisis de un programa de intervención [Social skills in the professional graduation of the psychologist: Analysis of an intervention program]. *Psicologia Conductual (Espanha), 7*(1), 27–47.
Del Prette, Z. A. P., & Del Prette, A. (2005). Psicologia das habilidades Sociais na Infância: Teoria e Prática [Psychology of social skills in childhood: Theory and practice] (1st. ed.). Petrópolis, Brazil: Vozes.
Del Prette, Z. A. P., & Del Prette, A. (2010). Habilidades Sociais e Análise do Comportamento: Proximidade histórica e atualidades [Social skills and behavior analysis: Historical connection and new issues]. *Perspectivas em Análise do Comportamento, 1*(2), 104–115.
Del Prette, Z. A. P., Del Prette, A., Gresham, F. M., & Vance, M. J. (2012). Role of social performance in predicting learning problems: Prediction of risk using logistic regression analysis. *School Psychology International Journal, 2*, 615–630.
Del Prette, Z. A. P.; Falcone, E. M. O., & Murta, S. G. (2013). Contribuições do campo das habilidades sociais para a compreensão, prevenção e tratamento dos transtornos de personalidade [The social skills field's contribution to the understanding, prevention and treatment of personality disorders]. In: L. F. Carvalho, & R. Primi. (Org.). *Perspectivas em psicologia dos transtornos da personalidade: Implicações teóricas e práticas [Different perspectives in psychology about personality disorders: Theoretical and practical implications].* (pp. 326–358). São Paulo, Brazil: Casa do Psicólogo.
Del Prette, Z. A. P., Rocha, M. M., & Del Prette, A. (2017). Programas de habilidades sociais na infância: Modelo triádico de intervenção com pais [Childhood social skills programs: Threefold mode of intervention with parents]. In: Petersen, C. & Wainer, P. *Terapia Cognitivo-Comportamental para Crianças e Adolescentes: Ciência e Arte [Cognitive Behavioral Therapy for Children and Adolescents: Science and Art].* (pp. 14–40). Porto Alegre, Brazil: Artmed.
Dowd, T., & Tierney, J. (2005). *Teaching social skills to youth: A step-by-step guide to 182 basic to complex skills plus helpful teaching techniques*. Crawford, Nebraska: Boys Town Press.
Elliott, S. M., & Gresham, F. M. (2007). *Classwide intervention program Teacher's guide*. Minneapolis, MN: NCS Pearson.
Greene, J. O., & Burleson, B. R. (Eds.). (2003). *Handbook of communication and social interaction skill*. Hoboken, NJ: Lawrence Earlbaum Associates Publishers.
Gresham, F. M. (2009). Análise do comportamento aplicada às habilidades sociais [Analysis of behavior applied to social skills] In: A. Del Prette, & Z. A. P. Del Prette (Orgs.), *Psicologia das habilidades sociais: Diversidade teórica e suas implicações [The Psychology of Social Skills: Theoretical Diversity and its Implications]* (pp. 17–66). Petrópolis: Vozes.
Hagar, K., Goldstein, S., & Brooks, R. (2006). *Seven steps to improve your child's social skills: Teaching social skills for children ages* (pp. 5–14). Plantation, FL: Speciality Press.
Hargie, O., Saunders, C., & Dickson, D. (1994). *Social skills in interpersonal communication* (3rd ed.). London/New York: Routledge.
Kestenberg, C. C. & Falcone, E. M. O. (2017). Programa de promoção de empatia para graduandos de enfermagem [Program for promoting empathy for nursing undergraduates]. Em *Psicologia das habilidades sociais: Diversidade teórica e suas implicações [The Psychology of Social Skills: Theoretical Diversity and its Implications].* (pp. 115–144). Petrópolis, Brazil: Vozes (1st ed.).

Lopes, D. C. (2013). Programa universal de habilidades sociais aplicado pelo professor: impacto sobre comportamentos sociais e acadêmicos [Universal social skills program applied by the teacher: *Impact on social and academic behaviors]* Graduate Program in Psychology, Universidade Federal de São Carlos.

Lopes, D. C., & Del Prette, Z. A. P. (2017). Programa multimídia de habilidades sociais para crianças (PMHSC) [Multimedia resources to teach social skills to children with low academic achievement (PHMSC)]. In: A. Del Prette, & Z. A. P. Prette (Orgs.). *Habilidades sociais: Intervenções efetivas em grupo [Social Skills: Effective Group Interventions]* (3ird. ed.) (pp. 145–174). São Paulo, Brazil: Casa do Psicólogo.

Monti, P. M., Kadden, R. M., Rohsenow, D. J., Cooney, N. L., & Abrams, D. B. (2005). *Tratando a dependência de álcool: Um guia para o Treinamento de Habilidades de enfrentamento [Treating Alcohol Dependence: A Guide to Coaching Skills Training]* (2nd ed.). São Paulo, Brazil: Roca.

Olaz, F. O., Medrano, L. A. & Cabanillas, G. A. (2017). Programa vivencial versus programa instrucional de habilidades sociais: impacto sobre a autoeficácia de universitários [Experiential program versus instructional social skills program: impact on university students´ self-efficacy]. In A. Del Prette, & Z. A. P. Prette, (Orgs.), *Habilidades sociais: Intervenções efetivas em grupo [Social Skills: Effective Group Interventions]* (3ird. ed.) (pp. 175–202). São Paulo, Brazil: Casa do Psicólogo.

Pereira, C. de S. (2010). *Habilidades sociais para o trabalho: Efeitos de um programa para jovens com deficiência física [A professional social skills program for unemployed people with physical disability: Needs, Process and effects].* Graduate Program in Special Education, Universidade Federal de São Carlos.

Pereira-Guizzo, C. S., & Del Prette, A. (2017). Programa de habilidades sociais profissionais para pessoas com deficiência física desempregadas [Professional social skills program for unemployed people with physical disabilities]. In: A. Del Prette, & Z. A. P. Prette, (Orgs.). *Habilidades sociais: Intervenções efetivas em grupo [Social Skills: Effective Group Interventions]* (3ird. ed.) (pp. 203–230). São Paulo, Brazil: Casa do Psicólogo.

Rocha, M. M. (2009). Programa de habilidades sociais educativas com pais: efeitos sobre o desempenho social e acadêmico de filhos com TDAH [Social skills program with parents: Effects over the social and academic performance of children with]. Graduate Program in Special Education, Universidade Federal de São Carlos.

Vila, E. M., & Del Prette, A. (2009). Relato de um programa de treinamento de habilidades sociais com professores de crianças com dificuldades de aprendizagem [Report of a social skills training program with teachers of children with learning difficulties]. In: S. R. de Souza, & V. B. Haydu. (Org.), *Psicologia Comportamental Aplicada: Avaliação e intervenção nas áreas do esporte, clínica, saúde e educação [Applied Behavioral Psychology: Assessment and Intervention in Sport, Clinical, Health and Education Areas]* (pp. 113–135). Londrina, Brazil: EDUEL.

Part II
Guidelines for Practice

Chapter 5
Evaluation

Abstract In this chapter we focus on the evaluation (initial, process, continuous, and final), highlighting the importance of the follow-up evaluation of the results obtained. From this perspective, the evaluation instruments and procedures usually used in Brazil are briefly presented. The importance of the procedures involved in each of these evaluations is briefly discussed.

Keywords Social skills evaluation · Assessment · Continuous evaluation · Follow-up · Brazilian SST scales · Evaluation procedures

5.1 Initial Evaluation: Why and What to Evaluate

The aim of the initial evaluation is to make a precise diagnosis of the client's complaints and should necessarily include (a) their deficits regarding the requisites for social competence, (b) their existing skills and abilities, and (c) competing behaviors and other factors related to disorders (e.g., anxiety). These aspects must be evaluated in relation to the client's day-to-day interpersonal tasks. The therapist should also investigate the presence or absence of psychological or psychiatric disorders, physical health, self-esteem, self-efficacy, NVPC, the client's evaluation of their relationships and quality of life, etc (Fig. 5.1).

Fig. 5.1 Initial evaluation

A client may often seek help concerning complaints that apparently do not include interpersonal difficulties. They can refer to insomnia, for example, or to feeling hurt when some colleagues appear indifferent to them, or also refer to favorable outcomes, achieved with great difficulty. It is important to investigate what the client does (behaviors) in relation to each aspect of the complaint in terms of frequency, duration, and contingencies associated to the

Z. A. P. Del Prette, A. Del Prette, *Social Competence and Social Skills*,
https://doi.org/10.1007/978-3-030-70127-7_5

complaint. Additionally, the therapist must ask for greater detailing of the activities the client considers *agreeable* or *disagreeable*. When focusing upon deficits in the requirements for the therapist can organize the obtained information or ask for further information that would allow the characterization of the client's repertoire in terms of self-monitoring, self-knowledge, knowledge of their environment, and their values.

This information may be enough for the therapist to identify, in terms of social competence, the existing skills and deficits the client has for dealing with another's undesired behaviors and their own, little accepted behaviors, or those with great response cost. The organization of this information in a portfolio for each client and/or group is important for when the program's objectives, structure, and procedures are defined. For individual interventions, the initial evaluation can be quite similar to that recommended for group SST programs. It also occurs before the intervention, and the client's portfolio can be carefully detailed.

5.1.1 How to Assess

The evaluation of social skills should be, insofar as possible, a multimodal evaluation (Del Prette & Del Prette, 2009, 2013; Del Prette, Monjas, & Caballo, 2006). This means evaluating through different instruments and procedures (interviews, inventories, checklists, direct observation, role-play, etc.) and gathering information with and from different informants: in the case of a child, with family members and teachers; in the case of an adult, with family members.

An interview can be especially important to identify a client's interpersonal difficulties and the pertinence, or not, of an SST program for them. An interview can be how the client and therapist first make contact and can be later complemented with other procedures and instruments for evaluation. Sometimes, it also can be used after an inventory is applied, as a way of detailing information about identified difficulties.

An excerpt from an evaluation interview follows with the therapist's speech indicated by the letter T and the client's with the letter C, with notes about the client's NVPC, as the T seeks to obtain information about any difficulties in social skills the client may be facing. While the information given during the interview is preliminary, it contains indicators that suggest the existence of interpersonal problems, reinforced by the observations about the client's behavior during the initial interview.

Excerpt from interview assessment

C: *My wife and I are always fighting… (avoids eye contact)*

T: *How long has this been going on?*

C: *Some six or seven months now. These days, I arrive home late to avoid the arguments, but it is no good…*

T: *When you arrive late, does she complain?*

C: *Yes… I try to explain it, but I can't… (looks towards the door)*

T: *What do you say?*

C: *I ask her to listen to me. She is quiet, but then I don't know what to say (looks to T)*

T: *[…]*

C: *The worst is that, at work, a colleague keeps teasing me…*

T: *What does he do?*

C: *Keeps making jokes… (crosses hands over legs)*

T: *What do you mean? […] What kind of jokes does he make?*

C: *He keeps imitating me and laughing*

T: *Have you spoken to him about this? (shakes head 'no')*

C: *I tried… and he said: Go ahead, man, tell me.*

T: *And…?*

C: *I said: Forget it… Gosh! I just noticed that in both cases I was furious and I didn't say anything…*

T: *Was there any situation in which you were able to say something?*

C: *I think… I tried, I tried…*

Using the initial interview as a base, the therapist can then use standardized instruments with the objective of characterizing types of social skills deficits, their possible generalization to other environments, competing behaviors, and the other requisites for social competence. Evaluation through interviews and inventories with other informants (parents, teachers, and classmates) is more common with children, as they can have difficulty with self-evaluations. Even with adults, however, other's reports (friends, partner, children, etc.) can sometimes help define more precisely the client's existing skills and deficits. In Brazil, there is a reasonable number of standardized instruments available for this, especially in the inventory and questionnaire categories (see http://www.rihs.ufscar.br/instrumentos-de-avaliacao-bl/; see also, e.g., Del Prette & Del Prette, 2009, 2013, 2019; Del Prette, Del Prette, & Peixoto, 2021); Gresham & Elliot, 2016).

Evaluation through reports should, whenever possible, be complemented with observation, which can involve (a) role-playing (structured or semi-structured, brief or extensive); (b) video recording inside homes, schools, hospitals, or other environments; (c) video records taken by the therapist or an assistant in the client's environment (most common with children in their homes, in schools, and/or in a penal institution); and (d) records made by the client, using worksheets. Table summarizes the main aspect to be assessed and the resources to do so. They consider both datasets obtained from personal accounts and those from direct observation or via structured situations (Table 5.1).

Table 5.1 Requisites for social competence and procedures for assessing them

Aspects to be assessed	How to assess
Social skills: Breadth and variability of repertoire, as well as which skills are presently deficient concerning the client's interpersonal tasks in family, work, leisure, and other contexts and competing behaviors	Self-report inventories and accounts from significant others provide a general evaluation that can then be detailed through interviews, structured or semi-structured role-playing situations, direct observation in a natural environment
Self-monitoring: Capacity to analyze the contingencies associated to their own behavior (antecedents or demands, consequences) and that of others	Interviews and role-play where the client and the therapist observe and analyze the client's behavior during the session
Knowledge of the environment: Capacity to identify the culture's norms, values, and rules for coexistence in different contexts and during different interpersonal tasks	Interviews and using a checklist or script during initial sessions
Self-knowledge: Capacity to identify one's own abilities (in terms of deficiencies and capabilities), beliefs, feelings, personal standards, self-efficacy, etc.	Self-report inventories and interviews, complemented by an evaluation by others, direct observation, and the client's account of his/her behavior
Values of coexistence: What the client values as desirable and correct about his/her own behavior and that of others and what he/she considers undesirable and incorrect	Interviews and questions to identify values and personal mores, for example, analysis of interpersonal situations, observations about the client's behavior within the group

Based on the information and indicators noted during the initial evaluation, the therapist can organize a client's portfolio. The portfolio identifies objectives relevant to the intervention and the monitoring of the client's acquisitions and improvements throughout the program.

5.2 Process Evaluation

The process evaluation must occur during the course of the program, be it in group or individual format, and it includes detailed information about the client's behaviors during the session and as evidenced by homework reports. Thus, it is important to collect information about the client's involvement, their partial improvements, and, also, any difficulties they might present.

In relation to the client's acquisitions, the process evaluation must go beyond direct in-session observation and seek indicatives of generalization of new social skills to environments outside of the session context, be it through the accounts of the client or of other informants (parents or guardian, for children). Concerning the program itself, it is important to register any changes or choices to maintain the initial plan and note any events that facilitated or made the progression of the program more difficult. Other things to register are using new resources or procedures, for example, the use of individual sessions for one or more client, alterations in the portfolio, and assigning additional homework.

In order to conduct a process evaluation, the therapist must keep a record of the relevant information at the end of each session, for example, of any acquisitions or difficulties observed, motivation, etc. This information can be complemented with data and the therapist's observations about attendance, collaboration during procedures, and spontaneous accounts, or in other words, behaviors characteristic to the therapeutic and to subjective well-being.

5.3 Continuous Evaluation

When the initial evaluation is based upon self-reports, both the existing skills and the deficits or difficulties can be over- or underestimated. Because of this, clients can start to relate acquisitions or difficulties during the initial sessions of an experiential program that had not been previously mentioned. Natural acquisitions may also occur by observing colleagues' behavior. This explains the importance of a continuous evaluation during the program.

The continuous evaluation is part of any intervention, and this also true for SST programs. Evaluation can be done through (a) direct observation and notes the therapist makes on the worksheets for each session; (b) specific evaluations made by other participants, whenever it is the case of a group SST program; (c) notes about the client's accounts, especially regarding interpersonal homework; and (d) evaluations from teachers, nurses, social workers, and employees, when the intervention happens at schools, hospitals, penal institutions, etc. This evaluation identifies acquisitions that indicate the overcoming of deficits and indicate generalization and even eventual new difficulties or deficits, not only in social skills but in the other requisites for social competence.

5.4 Final Evaluation

This evaluation seeks to ascertain the client's acquisitions during the program, comparing their behavior in final sessions with their initial repertoire, including their self-evaluation and that of others. Positive results can be taken as signs of the intervention's effectiveness and efficacy. This evaluation is preferably done using the same instruments used at the beginning of the intervention, including self-evaluation and that of others. In short, the final evaluation should measure any clinical or educationally relevant improvements in terms of:

- Overcoming initial deficits
- Reduction of behaviors that competed with socially skilled behavior
- Reduction of interpersonal symptoms associated to complaints or disorders

- Acquisition of new social skills
- Acquisition/perfecting of the other requirements for social competence
- Improvements in quality of life, self-esteem, resilience, happiness, and other indicators of the impacts the intervention might have had

As the final evaluation is related to process analyses, it can help improve the program, allowing the therapist to raise hypotheses about the effectiveness of the procedures and techniques in use and about the conditions in different moments of the program. For individual intervention, the therapist reevaluates the client mainly through direct observation and through reports from the client or other significant people. It is also beneficial, in this case, to do a comparative analysis with the initial repertoire and the process analysis.

5.4.1 Reporting Progress to Client

Client's progress report should focus upon initial information about their repertoire (existing abilities, deficits, difficulties, etc.), improvements and acquisitions that lead toward overcoming problems, and indicators of generalization. At the end of the program, the therapist should inform the client about the entirety of their acquisition and, should it be the case, objectives that have not yet been reached.

5.5 Follow-Up

This evaluation, carried out sometime after the program has finished (2 months or more), is important to verify if the acquisitions are being maintained. The evaluation should be previously discussed with the client in the form of one or more extra group meeting or individual sessions with this objective. Other resources may be used as well, such as contact by telephone or e-mail, questionnaires with only a few items, sent to teachers or parents, etc. This evaluation must not be left aside for individual intervention. It is a practice that is not yet used very much, even in research, but increasingly valued.

5.6 Generalization Evaluation

Generalization evaluation is articulated with the continuous and process evaluations in addition to the final and follow-up evaluations. It deserves special attention, as, ultimately, generalization is the main objective of any intervention. It is important to evaluate whether the acquired skills are being used as needed, in the natural environment: (a) in new situations and contexts, (b) with many different people, and (c) during interpersonal tasks that are similar to the training sessions when the skills were learned. In this case, the client's perceptions are also important for the therapist to assess response costs and to determine if the new social skills are accepted in the natural environment. It is important to remember that generalization must be monitored and assessed starting with the initial sessions and throughout the entirety of the program.

References

Del Prette, Z. A. P., & Del Prette, A. (2009). Avaliação de habilidades sociais: Bases conceituais, instrumentos e procedimentos [Assessing social skills: Conceptual basis, instruments and procedures] In: A. Del Prette, & Z. A. P. Del Prette (Orgs.), *Psicologia das habilidades sociais: Diversidade teórica e suas implicações [The psychology of social skills: Theoretical diversity and its implications]* (pp. 187–229). Petrópolis, Brazil: Vozes.

Del Prette, Z. A. P., & Del Prette, A. (2013). Social Skills Inventory (SSI-Del-Prette): Characteristics and studies in Brazil. In: F. L. Osório (Org.), *Social Anxiety Disorders: From Theory to Practice* (pp. 49–62). Nova Iorque, Brazil: Nova Science Publishers, ISBN 978-1-62417-826-9.

Del Prette, Z. A. P., & Del Prette, A. (2019). Instrumentos de avaliação de habilidades sociais no Brasil [*Social skills assessment instruments in Brazil].* In M. N. Baptista e cols. (Orgs). *Compêndio de Avaliação Psicológica [Psychological Assessment Compendium/* (pp. 376–396). Petrópolis, Brazil: Vozes. ISBN 978-85-326-6077-0.

Del Prette, Z. A. P., Del Prette, A., & Peixoto, E. M. (2021). Social Skills Inventory-2 Del-Prette: expanding and updating psychometric properties. Estudos de Psicologia (Campinas), 38, e190124. Epub August 24, 2020.

Del Prette, Z. A. P., Monjas, I., & Caballo, V. E. (2006). Evaluación de las habilidades sociales en niños [Evaluation of social skills in children] In: V. E. Caballo (Org.), *Manual para la evaluación clinica de los transtornos psicológicos [Manual for the cognitive-behavioral assessment of psychological disorders]* (pp. 373–399). Madrid, Spain: Pirámide.

Gresham, F. M. & Elliott, S. N. (2016). *Inventário de Habilidades Sociais, Problemas de Comportamento e Competência Acadêmica para Crianças: SSRS Manual de aplicação, Apuração e Interpretação* [Translated and adapted in Brazil by Z. A. P. Del Prette, Z. A. P., L. C. Freitas, M. Bandeira, M. & A. Del Prette]. São Paulo, Brazil: Pearson.

Chapter 6
Techniques, Procedures, and Resources Associated with Experiential Activities

Abstract In this chapter we initially describe the main techniques and resources common to Social Skills Training programs (feedback, reinforcement/shaping, modeling, cognitive restructuring, problem-solving). We emphasize the use of them in the context of experiential activities (as described in the Chap. 4), associated to interpersonal homework and instructional activities targeted to the requirements of social competence.

Keywords Social Skills Training · Experiential activities · Interpersonal homework · Interpersonal instruction · Techniques · Procedures

Experiential activities create a context in which a reasonable number of demands can be established for performances in need of improvement. They also create an opportunity for some participants' behaviors to serve as models or as an illustration of behavioral alternatives. These conditions, complemented using different procedures, techniques, and intervention resources, make it possible to promote variability in social skills. Depending on the repertoire and the needs of the participants, the program may include specific modules to reduce anxiety and for intervention on beliefs and private behaviors identified as dysfunctional for successful interactions.

Considering the effective practices in Social Skills Training emphasizing social competence, this chapter presents specific guidelines for techniques, resources, and other procedures that can be used in association with the experiential activities. Techniques such as instructional exercises, interactive instructions (II), behavioral rehearsal, and interpersonal homework can be used in SST programs. The procedure may also include using feedback, reinforcement, shaping, analyzing an interaction's contingencies, and modeling (real or symbolic). We highlight the potential benefits and pitfalls of using multimedia resources (when and how to use them), irrespective of whether they will be used in an SST program.

Z. A. P. Del Prette, A. Del Prette, *Social Competence and Social Skills*,
https://doi.org/10.1007/978-3-030-70127-7_6

6.1 Main Techniques and Procedures

The main techniques, procedures, and resources that can be used in group or individual SST programs are described below. They include those adopted by the authors (A. Del Prette & Del Prette, 2001, 2005, 2017; Z. Del Prette & Del Prette, 1999; 2005) and others from classical guides on Social Skills Training (e.g., Caballo, 2003; Curran & Monti, 1982, Dowd & Tierney, 2005; Elliott & Gresham, 2007; Goldstein, Sprafkin, Gershaw, & Klein, 1980). In each one, there is a brief description followed by guidelines on *how* and *when* they can be used.

Feedback Verbal description of the participant's behavior shortly after it happens. The therapist can provide feedback themselves or help participants give feedback, always focusing on positive feedback. Giving feedback on behaviors presented during the sessions is important for refining various skills, including those of describing behaviors and providing feedback.

Reinforcement and Shaping Reinforce successive approximations of the target behavior or ask group members to provide positive feedback to that end. Use this during sessions as contingently as possible for any acquisitions or improvement toward the behavioral objectives.

Modeling Request a participant to observe a model's behavior and imitate it, followed by feedback and/or a second attempt. Use mainly in case of difficulty with shaping behavior: one or more participants are asked to observe the behavior of another and then reproduce it.

Symbolic Modeling Request a participant to observe and imitate symbolic models such as characters from a story, dolls, puppets, etc. Use this when some difficulty in learning though shaping is noticed, especially with children; the child could be asked to verbalize what the character is doing as a way to help develop the target behavior.

Covert Modeling The therapist and client create an imaginary model; the therapist asks the client to *visualize* the model's behavior, describing their behaviors and the results obtained. It is used when the client has difficulty learning by shaping or when he/she shows imaginative resources that suggest this to be an effective and viable alternative.

Role-Playing Role-playing is a technique that involves simulating interactions in interpersonal tasks relevant to the client and which may include role reversal when the client assumes the role of the interlocutor. It is used when the client finds it difficult to report the interlocutor's behavior or to understand an interactive context and discriminate behaviors and contingencies (Fig. 6.1).

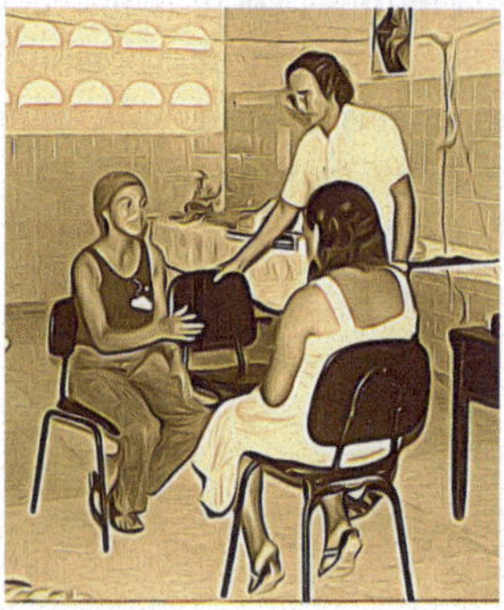

Fig. 6.1 Role-playing

Behavioral Rehearsal An arrangement of the session's interactive context (structured or minimally structured, involving other participants) that allows the client's behavior in rehearsals to be progressively improved. The situations created can be based on interpersonal homework accounts or on other difficulties reported with regard to specific tasks common to most of the participants.

Interpersonal Homework (IH) Assigning tasks that require putting skills into practice in interactive contexts and giving clear and concise instructions for the participants to complete outside the session. They are attributed at the end of each session and described and analyzed at the beginning of the following session (detailed procedure below).

Cognitive Restructuring Asking questions and having the participant analyze dysfunctional beliefs, which involve overreactions, overgeneralizations, self-deprecating statements, etc. This technique may be adopted for cases in which a participant reports beliefs or rules that show evidence that they are avoiding or escaping engaging in necessary behaviors opposite to competing behaviors.

Problem-Solving Inducing a metacognitive process for understanding and solving problems that follows these steps: (1) define the problem, (2) generate/devise alternative solutions, (3) evaluate each alternative, (4) select one of them, (5) implement the chosen solution, and (6) follow up on the effectiveness of chosen alternative. It can be used when a client needs to solve a problem and has difficulty analyzing it and identifying possible solutions; it can be used individually or in a group decision-making process.

Contingency Analysis Requests to identify relationships between behavior (observed or reported) and their antecedents and consequences. Conduct more intensively in the initial sessions and gradually encourage the participant's spontaneous use and increasingly more refined analyses.

Interactive Instruction (II) A moment in which the therapist or facilitator interactively discusses with and teaches the participants important aspects of social competence (situations, demands, culture norms, values, behavioral contingencies, and others). It is recommended to use alongside other procedures and resources but to a lesser extent than other procedures, prioritizing the client's behavior.

Instructional Exercises Paper and pencil tasks for analyses, applying concepts, exemplification, developing answers, illustrations, etc. They are used in articulation with II in sessions and/or as tasks outside the session.

Using Multimedia Resources Using texts, films, messages, music, and other resources that illustrate socially competent or noncompetent interactions and their consequences. They are used mainly to illustrate performances for subsequent analysis and reflection, for modeling, and for supporting II.

6.2 Describing Some Techniques and Procedures

Some of the techniques and procedures described in this chapter, though important in SST programs, are not usually emphasized in technical manuals and are therefore presented in more detail below.

6.2.1 *Interpersonal Homework*

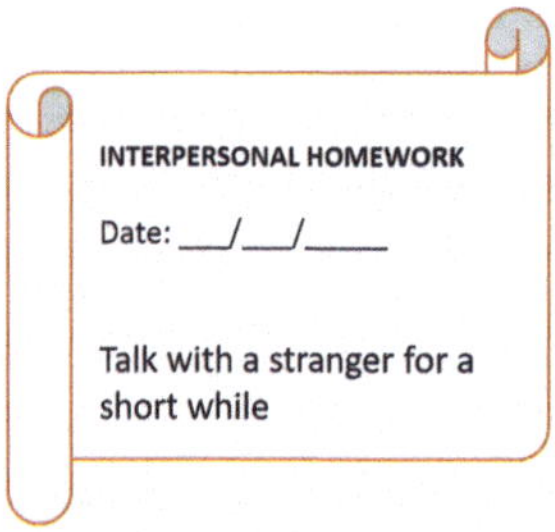

Fig. 6.2 An interpersonal homework

Experiential activity programs also allow for the use of interpersonal homework (IH) from the first session onwards, unless specific conditions make it difficult. The type of task assigned depends on the participants' psychological and social resources and should meet several objectives besides those usually associated with this technique. Some tasks may provide relevant information to adjust the program to the needs of the group (A. Del Prette & Del Prette, 2005, 2017) (Fig. 6.2).

In general terms, IH objectives include experiences outside the sessions (doing the task) and within the sessions (recounting the experience, analyzing and evaluating one's own tasks, and taking part in analyzing tasks reported by peers in group programs). These conditions are expected to be favorable for:

- Generalizing new social skills, learned during sessions, for other environments and interlocutors
- Exercising self-monitoring components, such as observing, describing, and analyzing contingencies in the natural context
- Experimenting with environmental contingencies, improving sensitivity toward them
- Listening to evaluations and feedback given by the facilitator or group members regarding one's attempts at practicing new skills and also provide feedback to others
- Evaluating whether acquisitions are sufficient to deal with the interactive demands of their daily lives
- Describing contingencies identified in another participant's report of a task, in terms of consequences versus the cost of accomplishing them

The figure shows some suggestions of generic interpersonal homework. However, the list for each group should be tailored according to the needs identified in the portfolio and converted into client's objectives. Assuming, for example, that some participants show self-control difficulties, the facilitator can assign tasks in which self-control is a necessary skill to complete the task, giving them a chance to practice it. By examining the IH table, the reader will identify at least two tasks related to self-control (Fig. 6.3).

In the initial phase of the program, the same tasks, thus called generic tasks, are assigned for all participants. Using generic tasks makes it easier to level out the repertoire of the group and correct discrepancies. In the following sessions, the therapist then assigns personalized tasks, that is, tailored to suit the needs of each participant or, alternatively, assign the same task to small groups that share similar difficulties.

EXAMPLES OF INTERPERSONAL HOMEWORK

- ✓ Talk with strangers in a risk-free public environment (pharmacy, bakery, shopping mall).
- ✓ Do not answer a friend´s question.
- ✓ Praise a colleague's accessory or clothing.
- ✓ Ask a non-abusive favor to a colleague;
- ✓ Hug a family member or friend.
- ✓ Request a change of subject in a conversation.
- ✓ Refuse an order.
- ✓ Do not answer an intrusive question.
- ✓ Leave a situation similar to one in which you usually lose control.

Fig. 6.3 Examples of interpersonal homework

In general, clients, both in group and in individual intervention, like doing IH; however, there may be some occasions in which they do not complete the activity. The most common justifications are (a) lack of opportunity; (b) forgetfulness; (c) self-evaluation of not having the skills required for the social task; and (d) remembering similar activities done well before the task was requested, as shown in the illustration. Items a and b are the most common and can, with rare exceptions, be understood as avoidance behaviors or as a result of a true difficulty to complete the task (Fig. 6.4).

Fig. 6.4 Interpersonal homework reports

In addition to being attentive to the need of adjusting the complexity of the task to the client's repertoire, some procedures are useful to avoid these justifications and increase the probability of the participants finishing the task. The first procedure is to allow an extra week for the task to be finished, thus resulting in two tasks in the same week. The second procedure, related to forgetfulness, is to instruct participants, already in the first session of the program, to use mnemonic resources (reminders). Clarify that it should be a stimulus present in the environments in which the task can be performed, and ask for examples of mnemonics that the participants usually use. Regarding the lack of opportunity, the therapist can ask participants to closely observe the contexts in which the required scenarios are likely to occur and to guide them to create opportunities using questions or comments.

6.2.2 *Using Multimedia Resources*

Fig. 6.5 Multimedia resources

Multimedia resources are the products of literature (books, stories, short stories, comics, etc.), educational videos, movies, games, and various illustrations. Recently, they have been selected, planned, and used to support educational and therapeutic processes with children and adults. Some studies illustrate these resources, though not exhaustively (Casagrande, Del Prette, & Del Prette, 2013; Comodo, Del Prette, Del Prette, & Manólio, 2011; Z. Del Prette & Del Prette, 2005; Del Prette, Domeniconi, Amaro, Laurenti, Benitez, & Del Prette, 2012; Dias, Del Prette, & Del Prette, 2019; Lopes, Del Prette, & Del Prette, 2013) (Fig. 6.5).

Choosing multimedia resources should be part of the therapist's activities, during which he/she should consider the objectives those resources will help achieve. In general, multimedia resources can bring relevant information about the rules and values of the social context, as well as illustrations that serve as symbolic models of social skills, especially with children.

Videos, movies, and other multimedia materials are excellent resources to be included in the SST programs. Commercial films do not usually have educational pretensions but contain potentially educational excerpts that can be edited and used.

Resources should not be confused with *techniques*: they are props that depend on the therapist's or facilitator's skills to use them in order to help the participants to be motivated and learn.

6.2.3 Instructional Activities

Instructional activities are a complement to experiential activity programs. They should be used sparingly, but they may occur at various points in an SST program.

A procedure foreseen and used as brief interludes is the II. In this procedure, the therapist can produce short texts for the participants to read and then have a discussion, briefly present the content with the support of visual resources, or even combine these procedures. In the experiential activity *Practicing Feedback* (Chap. 10), a supporting text and a set of slides are presented to support this activity. Some important recommendations for using II are as follows:

- Engage the group in a discussion group so that everyone participates.
- Avoid going on for too long; the maximum time should be restricted to about 20 min or less depending on the clientele.
- Avoid opposing the beliefs of the participants, waiting for a suitable moment for clarification, when applicable.

Another instructional procedure is to organize the participants so as to analyze situations (written down) or answer questions about a text. They may complete this task individually or in small groups and then present it to the larger group. This also helps to practice public speaking. These exercises should be immediately followed by feedback from the therapist or other participants. As an example, Chap. 10 describes some exercises of this kind for understanding and practicing assertiveness and empathy. These resources are useful to both individual and group interventions.

References

Caballo, V. E. (2003). *Manual de avaliação e treinamento das habilidades sociais [Social Skills Training and Assessment Manual]*. São Paulo, Brazil: Santos.

Casagrande, A. P., Del Prette, A., & Del Prette, Z. A. P. (2013). *Brincando e aprendendo Habilidades Sociais [Playing and Learning Social Skills]*. Jundiaí, Brazil: Paco Editorial.

Comodo, C. N., Del Prette, A., Del Prette, Z. A. P., & Manólio, C. L. (in memoriam), (2011). O Passeio de Bia (vídeo): Apresentação e validade interna e externa de um recurso para a promoção de habilidades sociais de pré-escolares [Bia walk (video): presentation and internal and external validity of a resource to promote social skills of preschoolers]. *Psicologia: Teoria e Prática, 13*(1), 34–47.

Curran, J. P., & Monti, P. M. (1982). *Social skills training: A practical handbook for assessment and treatment*. New York: The Guilford Press.

Del Prette, A., & Del Prette, Z. A. P. (2001). *Psicologia das relações interpessoais e habilidades sociais: Vivências para o trabalho em grupo [The Psychology of Interpersonal Relationships and Social Skills: Experiential Activities for Groups]* (1st ed.). Petrópolis, Brazil: Vozes.

Del Prette, A., & Del Prette, Z. A. P. (2005). A importância das tarefas de casa como procedimento para a generalização e validação do treinamento de habilidades sociais. In: J. H. Guilhardi, & N. C. Aguirre (Orgs.), *Primeiros passos em Análise do Comportamento e Cognição [First steps in the Analysis of Behavior and Cognition]* (pp. 67–74). Santo André, Brazil: ESETec.

Del Prette, A., & Del Prette, Z. A. P. (Orgs), (2017). *Habilidades Sociais: Intervenções efetivas em grupo [Social Skills: Effective Group Interventions]* (3ird. ed.). São Paulo, Brazil: Casa do Psicólogo (3ª. ed.).

Del Prette, Z. A. P., & Del Prette, A. (1999). *Psicologia das Habilidades Sociais: Terapia, Educação e Trabalho [The Psychology of Social Skills: Therapy, Education and Work]* (1st ed.). Petrópolis (SP), Brazil: Vozes.

Del Prette, Z. A. P., & Del Prette, A. (2005). Psicologia das habilidades Sociais na Infância: Teoria e Prática [Psychology of Social Skills in Childhood: Theory and Practice] (1st.Ed.). Petrópolis (SP), Brazil: Vozes.

Del Prette, Z. A. P., Domeniconi, C., Amaro, L., Laurenti, A., Benitez, P., & Del Prette, A. (2012). Tolerância e respeito às diferenças: Efeitos de uma atividade educativa a escola [Tolerance and respect for differences: The effects of an educational activity at school]. *Psicologia: Teoria e Prática, 14*(1), 168–182.

Dias, T. P., Casali, I. G., Del Prette, A., & Del Prette, Z. A. P. (2019). Automonitoria en el campo de las Habilidades Sociales: Especificación de sus indicadores conductuales [Self-monitoring in the field of social skills: Specification of behavioral indicators]. *Acta Comportamentalia, 27*(3), 3.

Dowd, T., & Tierney, J. (2005). *Teaching social skills to youth: A step-by-step guide to 182 basic to complex skills plus helpful teaching techniques*. Crawford, Nebraska: Boys Town Press.

Elliott, S. M., & Gresham, F. M. (2007). *Classwide intervention program Teacher's guide*. Minneapolis, MN: NCS Pearson.

Goldstein, A. P., Sprafkin, R. P., Gershaw, N. J., & e Klein, P. (1980). *Skillstreaming the adolescent: A structured approach to teaching prosocial skills*. Champaign, IL: Research Press Company.

Lopes, D. C., Del Prette, Z. A. P., & Del Prette, A. (2013). Recursos multimídia no ensino de habilidades sociais a crianças de baixo rendimento acadêmico [Multimedia resources to teach social skills to children with low academic achievement]. *Psicologia: Reflexão eCrítica, 26*(3), 451–458.

Chapter 7
How to Promote Social Competence Requirements

Abstract In this chapter, we present specific practical strategies to promote specific requirements of social competence: social skills variability, self-monitoring and contingency analysis skills, knowledge about the social environment, values of coexistence, and self-knowledge. Besides the techniques and resources presented in Chap. 6, we emphasize experiential activities, interpersonal homework, and instructional activities.

Keywords Social competence · Social skills variability · Self-monitoring · Contingency analysis · Values of coexistence · Self-knowledge

Except for social skills, the other requirements of social competence have not received due attention in interpersonal training programs. So we propose some alternatives to improve the variability of social skills, self-monitoring and contingency analysis skills, knowledge about the social environment, values of coexistence, and self-knowledge. In general, guidelines are based on resources and techniques presented in Chap. 6 (reinforcing, modeling, shaping, giving feedback, cognitive restructuring, etc.) and three main procedures, experiential activities, interpersonal homework, and instructional activities (Del Prette & Del Prette, 1999, 2001, 2005, 2017), here applied to those requirements of social competence.

7.1 Variability of Social Skills

Using experiential activities is an especially favorable technique for promoting behavioral variability. In both group situations and individual intervention, the client has contact with the contingencies of the interpersonal tasks as mediated by the therapist. They are asked to describe their behavior and identify antecedents and consequences. Experiential activities are a good opportunity for learning behavioral variability even when the activity was not planned to promote it. The following examples of a therapist's actions are valid for group interventions but can also be adjusted to individual format:

Z. A. P. Del Prette, A. Del Prette, *Social Competence and Social Skills*,
https://doi.org/10.1007/978-3-030-70127-7_7

- Request the participant to repeat the previous activity, this time presenting different behaviors.
- Instruct the interlocutors (who are also part of the Experiential Group (EG)) to react differentially in accordance with the quality of the alternative presented by the participant.
- Choose members of the Observer Group (OG) to provide positive feedback about the behaviors more likely to result in favorable consequences considering the experiential situation's demands.

The direct exposure of the client to the conditions and effects of their behavior, directly in session or reported during a homework assignment, can also increase their sensibility to contingencies. This happens because of the training in observation and contingency analysis, which favors:

- Testing variations of the same skill and the consequences associated to the differences in behavior and contingencies, even the most subtle ones
- Discriminating which adaptations are necessary to behaviors when faced with different demands and contexts, for example, family context, work, study, leisure, etc.

7.2 Self-Monitoring and Contingency Analysis

When conducting an experiential activity, the therapist has many opportunities to help participants learn self-monitoring. A simple way of doing this is interrupting an activity and asking the participant to:

- Describe their behavior up until that moment
- Describe the context and the interlocutor's behaviors (verbal and nonverbal)
- Evaluate if their behaviors have altered or not the course of the interaction in the intended direction
- List alternatives for the next step in the interaction and the probable consequences of each one
- Say what they have decided to do next

The participants of the OG can also be asked to make similar analyses either at some point during the experiential activity or at the end of it. This is an arrangement that keeps the members of the OG attentive and observant, increasing therefore the probability of learning through modeling. It is also possible and viable to ask for a contingency analysis of the interactions observed immediately before the activity.

For example, during one intervention, one of the participants had a pattern of speaking about illnesses whenever she found an opportunity to do so, which made her uninteresting to her interlocutors. In this case, a conversation was held with the client and the other members of the group discussing strategies for obtaining attention, which included behaviors such as complaining about illnesses. The members of the group agreed that this was a way of obtaining attention, but only for a short period of time, for it quickly produces distancing and avoidance in others. After the discussion, the therapist organized a role-play in which one of the members of the interacting group was instructed to complain about illness and the participant was asked to change the topic of conversation as soon as possible. With some initial difficulty, the client succeeded in changing the subject, receiving the approval of the others. The therapist assigned her, as IH (interpersonal homework), the task of listing different conversation topics and changing the subject when someone began discussing illnesses or medicines. This practice was successful, and the client started to have more interesting conversations, which could also be observed during the sessions.

As another example, with preschoolers, Dias and Del Prette (2015) describe the conditions and acquisitions of a group that participated in an intervention focused specifically on encouraging self-monitoring, using playful resources that illustrated interactions. The child was asked to identify which illustrations represented their usual way of behaving and to predict the consequences of different social behaviors and also received a complementary training in planned situations with demands directed toward practicing self-monitoring.

Adopting new behavior generally implies the ability to control impulses to respond in the usual manner and the capacity to formulate varied options and observe their effect. For many people, the greatest difficulty is, precisely, to *break habits*, which should then be the focus of the therapist's attention.

7.3 Knowledge About the Social Environment

In SST programs which work in group format, each group can be considered as a microcosm of the social environment because the participants bring with them, to the context of the session, various rules and norms from their environments, which are essential to the evaluation, acquisition, and generalization of their social skills.

During an experiential activity, the participants (EG) reproduce, analogously or symbolically, rules and norms present in the environments they live in. The EG participants also reflect, in their analysis and feedback, the rules and norms of the group's subculture. It is the therapist's task, therefore, to maximize these conditions. Some possibilities are suggested:

- Analyze or ask one of the participants to analyze the relationships between the explicit and implicit contingencies of the activity and the EG participants' behaviors.
- Ask participants to predict probable effects, in their natural environment, hypothetically caused by the EG's behaviors (*Olga, if you do this when you speak with your mother, how do you think she will react? And other group members, what do you think?*)
- Request that one participant identifies demands for the EG's behaviors (*In which situations of Olga's life could she act like this?*)

- Have an EG participant self-evaluate their behavior.
- Provide consequences (compliments and positive feedback) for the participants' acquisitions.

Thus, the probable effects of certain behavioral options, in the client's natural environment, are tested in the contexts of a session. This happens when the participants assess, or are asked to assess, a colleague's behavior while they are practicing. This allows everyone's knowledge about an environment's values and norms to increase. These exercises, along with the report about interpersonal homework, constitute, therefore, favorable conditions to improve a client's knowledge about which behavioral patterns are expected, tolerated, or rejected by the social environment and the group's subculture.

The identification and analysis of rules and norms, articulated to homework, can lead to the acceptance or rejection of these rules; in the second case, assertive confrontation skills may be required, in accordance with the criteria for social competence.

The knowledge to be acquired about the environment includes information on which behaviors are approved, rejected, and tolerated within his/her culture and according to each situation he/she is faced with. This information must be considered in light of the practical and ethical criteria for social competence. For this, the therapist can lead and mediate instructional activities, such as:

- Reflection on the tasks and interpersonal relationships in the participants' historical-cultural context.
- Analyze the interactions seen in session, or brought to it through a personal account, considering the existing patterns of coexistence and the criteria for social competence.
- Recognize socially established rights and situations in which they are violated, considering the historical process through which those interpersonal rights were won.

Interpersonal homework assignments are an important factor for expanding this kind of knowledge. Tasks that involve demands for assertive skills and empathic skills, for approaching someone in an affectionate and sexual way, for requesting an increase in salary, for collaborating in charity campaigns, interacting with authorities, etc., are examples of contexts which create conditions for these analyses.

7.4 Values of Coexistence

Values should be taught and developed from an early age. Thus, parents' and teachers' and other educators' actions are fundamental. Some educational experiences at schools have shown promise in this direction (e.g., Borges & Marturano, 2012).

When a person's values are incompatible with the notion of social competence, it is important to include and promote social competence during SST programs, even if the scope of such programs could be insufficient to alter those values significantly. For these cases, the experiential method is recommended because it facilitates shifting the focus from individuals to the group and the social context. For example, the experiential activity *Social Interaction Values* (Chap. 10) uses a metaphor to illustrate social values relevant to social interactions and helps participants to reflect on the implications of responsible social interactions. Additionally, the activity called *Joana's story*[1] sparks a discussion about how we may inadvertently let ourselves be taken in with preconceived ideas rather than an objective analysis of behaviors and contingencies. It shows evidence of the negative bias or prejudices often encountered by others who may behave differently and how this affects the quality of interpersonal relationships.

Activities that involve analyses and reflection (such as instructional exercises with written texts, interactive instructions, assigned reading, etc.) can also be oriented toward encouraging values of coexistence. In this case, it is a matter of increasing the participants' competence to analyze, estimate, or predict the consequences of different options of behavior and to infer favorable and unfavorable conditions for healthy interactions.

The ethical dimension of social competence encompasses, whenever possible, both sides of an interaction, be it an interaction between two people, different groups, or even broader and more complex social groups. In the first two cases, those involved are the individual (and participant in the intervention) and the group they are inserted into or their group in relation to another group. This proposal is coherent with the *win-win* principle, with respect to interpersonal rights and with the Golden Rule, which is at the base of social competence. Regarding issues related to broader contexts, such as belonging to different religions, sports teams, political parties etc., the guiding principle should be one of respecting differences.

In short, valuing healthy patterns of coexistence, compatible with socially competent behaviors, should be a goal present throughout the entire program. For this, it is essential that, whenever an opportunity arises, the therapist must direct the group's attention to identifying and analyzing the criteria for social competence pertinent to the ethical dimension and even providing a model or example of ethical positions.

---

[1] There is a version of this experiential activity for children and young adults called *Let's get to know Peter*.

7.5 Self-Knowledge

The experiential activity context is especially favorable for building self-knowledge. The therapist can maximize this possibility by:

- Bringing attention to the relationship between the participant's behavior and the immediate contingencies of the experiential activity (demands or antecedents and consequences)
- Mediating the OG's analyses and feedback about the relationship between the participant's behavior and the activity's contingencies
- Requesting the participant to describe their covert behaviors (such as thoughts and emotions) during an experiential activity

Differently from the accounts about interactions outside the sessions, accounts within the experiential context are probably more dependable, since they are requested immediately after the behavior they refer to took place. This leads to less reliance on memorization and allows the consistency between participants and what they most value to be verified. It is, therefore, a privileged environment to perfect the skill to relate events according to what was actually observed, allowing the facilitator to *calibrate* the correspondence between what the participant relates and the behaviors to which their account referred to. Giving an account of behaviors and the respective contingencies that preceded and follow social behaviors (three-term contingency) is an important step in the direction of self-knowledge and self-monitoring.

Some experiential activities are directed toward self-knowledge. In Chap. 10, *The silence game, Self-evaluation, Self-knowledge, Dealing with worry and stress* are some of the activities of note. In all of them, analyses are focused on one's own social repertoire, including the NVPC and private components of this behavior.

Assigning and analyzing interpersonal homework are also important strategies for increasing knowledge about the environment and the participant's own deficits and existing abilities. Thus, sometimes some participants are surprised about their own difficulty with apparently simple tasks or when they find easy tasks that others found more complex, thus developing more precision in terms of their self-knowledge.

References

Borges, D. S. C., & Marturano, E. M. (2012). *Alfabetização em valores humanos: Um método para o ensino de habilidades sociais [Literacy in human values: A method to teach social skills]*. São Paulo, Brazil: Summus.

Del Prette, A., & Del Prette, Z. A. P. (2001). *Psicologia das relações interpessoais e habilidades sociais: Vivências para o trabalho em grupo [The Psychology of Interpersonal Relationships and Social Skills: Experiential Activities for Groups]* (1st ed.). Petrópolis (SP), Brazil: Vozes.

Del Prette, A., & Del Prette, Z. A. P. (Orgs), (2017). *Habilidades Sociais: Intervenções efetivas em grupo [Social Skills: Effective Group Interventions]* (3ird. ed.). São Paulo, Brazil: Casa do Psicólogo (1ª. ed.).

Del Prette, Z. A. P., & Del Prette, A. (1999). *Psicologia das Habilidades Sociais: Terapia, Educação e Trabalho [The psychology of social skills: Therapy, education and work]* (1st ed.). Petrópolis (SP), Brazil: Vozes.

Del Prette, Z. A. P., & Del Prette, A. (2005). *Psicologia das habilidades Sociais na Infância: Teoria e Prática [Psychology of Social Skills in Childhood: Theory and Practice]* (1st ed.). Petrópolis (SP), Brazil: Vozes.

Dias, T. P., & Del Prette, Z. A. P. (2015). Promoção de automonitoria em crianças pré-escolares: impacto sobre o repertório social [Improving self-monitoring in preschoolers: Impact on the social repertoire]. *Acta Comportamentalia, 23*, 273–287.

Part III
Planning and Conducting Practice

Chapter 8
Planning a Social Skills Program Targeted at Social Competence

Abstract This chapter deals with planning programs to promote social competence and its requirements in group and individual formats. In order to do this, after considering structural and formal aspects of a program, we highlight the special care taken and guidelines to define the relevant objectives of intervention with clients, planning the main goals of sessions along the program, the generalization, and the structure of a typical session of training.

Keywords Social skills program · Planning sessions · Generalization · Program structure

Planning should be flexible to allow adjustments throughout the sessions.

Planning a program is an essential part of its effectiveness. A good plan presupposes (a) clarity regarding the rationale behind the program and its characteristics (what it is, for which situations it is recommended, its underlying theoretical base, procedures, etc.); (b) participant's characteristics, in terms of needs and resources, based upon careful assessment; (c) organized and defined objectives, based upon a portfolio; and (d) foreseen conditions for intervention that allow those objectives to be fulfilled.

This chapter details the stages for planning an experiential SST program with a preventative focus targeted toward adolescents and young adults.

- Definition of program objectives, including requisites for social competence and generalization
- Pacing objectives throughout the program's sessions
- Planning some initial, intermediary, and final sessions for the program

Preceding these aspects, an expectation regarding structure and formal characteristics can also contribute to good planning. Thus, the chapter will begin with these aspects.

Z. A. P. Del Prette, A. Del Prette, *Social Competence and Social Skills*,
https://doi.org/10.1007/978-3-030-70127-7_8

8.1 Structure of SST Experiential Programs

Several structural aspects of an experiential SST program, in group format, need to be previously defined. Among the basic items are (a) the number of participants and their characteristics, (b) physical environment, (c) desired/viable duration of the program and sessions, and (d) participation or not of a co-therapist. They are applied to almost all kinds and ages of participants (A. Del Prette & Del Prette, 2001, 2017; Z. Del Prette & Del Prette, 1999, 2005).

8.1.1 Number of Participants and Their Characteristics

Fig. 8.1 Number of participants in the program

The analyses of SST programs, available in the literature, show that they have many points in common but also some differences. Therapeutic programs differentiate themselves chiefly due to the patients' diagnoses (e.g., autism spectrum disorder, depression, schizophrenia, chemical dependence, behavioral problems, etc.), and among the other types of programs, the differences are mostly associated to sociodemographic characteristics (such as gender, age, educational level, type of job, etc.). Despite this variety, some of the structural characteristics they share are specified in publications (Fig. 8.1).

Therapeutic programs, in general, must be smaller (e.g., people diagnosed with schizophrenia), while preventative groups (promoting health within a group of adolescents) or professional groups (people seeking jobs) can be larger. When clients agree to group interventions, factors such as age, gender, and type of problem must be considered when creating the group. For example, a group for young people who have trouble with shyness could be bigger (8 to 12 participants). When trying to determine the ideal composition of the group, the therapist must also take into account how much individual attention each participant requires and if they have the support from a co-therapist or not.

Preventative and professional programs are, in general, conducted in larger groups, with about 30 participants or more, as can be the case with interventions in companies, schools, syndicates, etc. In these programs, the heterogeneity of the clientele can be an advantage, since it enables contact between people with different repertoires related to differences in gender, age, socioeconomical and educational conditions, social roles, previous repertoire, etc.

An alternative, which has not been explored much yet, is thematic groups, for example, focused on certain social skills (speaking in public, job interviews, refusing illegal drugs, managing teams at work, etc.), interpersonal tasks specific to certain stages of life (marital social skills, educational social skills for parents or teachers, preparing for retirement, assertiveness in older people, etc.), or even associated to specific disorders or problems (anger/aggressiveness, shyness, depression, learning difficulties, etc.)

8.1.2 Physical Environment

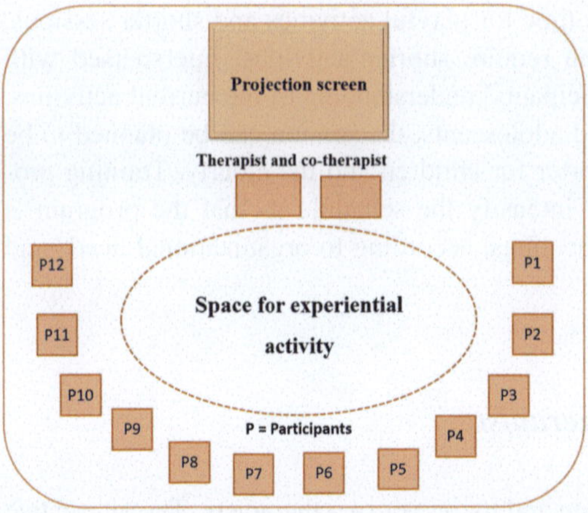

Fig. 8.2 Physical environment of an SST group program

The physical environment for group intervention should be organized so as to create conditions favorable for its success. Some elements of a group context are illustrated in Fig. 8.2. This setting was designed for groups with 8 to 12 participants; other layouts are possible, however, depending upon the space available and the number of participants. As illustrated, this setting allows:

- Eye contact between the therapist and every participant
- Eye contact among the group's members
- Chairs that can be easily moved to create different experiential activity arrangements
- Clear space for experiential activities
- Use of audio and visual equipment for instructional presentations, music and videos, etc.

8.1.3 Initial Contract

The initial contract comprises a spoken or written agreement about services provided by a therapist to a client. In a clinical intervention context, the contract is generally conducted by the secretary and must be established before the first session. The contract specifies the nature of the services provided, each party's commitments, and the rules for the intervention, such as what time it starts and ends, which days, etc. In a school context, or in any other kind of institution attending minors, the contract includes the parent's or guardian's written permission.

8.1.4 Program Length and Sessions

Predicting the duration of an SST program, both in group and individual format, is not an easy task. It depends on how frequent and how long the meetings are, as well as the information gathered in the initial assessment in terms of the extent of the existing resources and deficits in social skills and other requirements for social competence the participants might have.

Groups of children require more time for playful activities and shorter sessions, while groups of elderly people can require shorter activities, interspersed with pauses and checking up on the participants' understanding of the current activities. For group programs with adults and adolescents, the session can be planned to be around 2 h long. They must be shorter for children and the elderly. Training programs within companies generally intensify the schedule so that the program is carried out over fewer but longer meetings, according to organizational needs and availability.

8.1.5 Participation of Co-therapist

Sessions for group SST can be conducted by one or two therapists. The alternative with two therapists can have good results because:

- It optimizes session time, creating the possibility of dividing the group into smaller teams with similar activities.
- It allows the therapists to share impressions and thoughts, as well as share tasks such as recording sessions or other between-session activities (e.g., assessment and planning).

Involving family members can be positive both in group and individual settings, especially parents, whether they get help from another professional or not. Concerning the therapist(s), formal training cannot be dispensed, whether regarding therapeutic techniques or an understanding of the theoretical and practical aspects of SST. Preventative programs can be conducted by a facilitator, as long as they are supervised by a psychologist.

8.2 Defining the Objectives of the Program

Fig. 8.3 Defining objectives for a SST program

Defining objectives, for the group and for each client, is indispensable for selecting procedures and monitoring the results of an SST program. The objectives should be derived from the initial assessment, with due consideration to relevance and urgency. Intervention work should prioritize those social skills relevant to the client, considering the interpersonal tasks they face in their day-to-day life and potential improvements to their quality of life (Fig. 8.3).

As previously discussed, when the idea of social competence is the guiding principle of the program, the objectives necessarily must include requisites for it. This assessment should identify the following:

- Main social roles and interpersonal tasks in the client's day-to-day life
- Deficits and existing abilities in social skills, as indicated in their portfolio
- Behaviors that compete with the acquisition of social skills
- Problems and potentialities regarding the other requirements for social competence

With this *raw data*, objectives can be established that are relevant to an SST program. When competing behaviors are present, the therapist may decide to not include them as a direct target of the program in favor of improving the social skills that will *substitute* them. For example, aggressiveness can be reduced by promoting skills associated to empathy, self-monitoring, and expressing positive emotions; *impulsiveness* can be reduced in frequency and intensity by developing skills for self-control and solving interpersonal problems. In other words, instead of prioritizing excess behaviors, the therapist can focus on their counterpart, the deficits of behavior.

In group programs, the full set of objectives might include some that are common among two or more participants and others that are specific to each of them. To combine these two sets, the following steps are recommended:

- List the relevant interpersonal tasks common to all the participants or to small groups.
- Identify which deficits and existing skills regarding social skills and other requirements for social competence are found in individuals and which are shared by most of the group.
- Convert shared deficits into common objectives, considering both social skills and other requirements for social competence.
- Organize the group's objectives in increasing order of complexity, considering both social skills and other requirements for social competence.

- As the sessions proceed, use the continuous assessments and process assessments to revisit the need to include new objectives for certain participants and/or exclude objectives that already have been reached.

When the portfolio analysis shows that some skills are deficient for most participants in a group, they may be the target of special sessions for everyone to acquire these social skills. In general, participants share deficits in some NVPC, and in some basic, empathic, assertive, or problem-solving skills, justifying dedicating sessions specifically to overcoming a deficit that challenges the entire group. Even the participants that do not present a deficit properly can benefit greatly from perfecting these skills.

8.3 Pacing Objectives in Program Sessions

Generally, experiential SST programs, organized in a group format, for individuals without psychological disorders, are most effective with 15–18 participants, meeting twice a week. However, it must be emphasized that the program should run until any significant deficits have been overcome. In the case of preventative and professional programs, the duration shall assuredly be shorter, depending on the objectives established (Fig. 8.4).

Fig. 8.4 Pacing objectives of a SST program

Taking as an example a 12-session long, preventative SST program in group format, Fig. 8.5 shows a proposal for how the objectives should be organized. In this proposal, four sessions are set aside for the initial phase objectives, five for intermediary objectives, and three for final sessions. This organization is merely a suggestion that might facilitate the task of planning a program for the therapist, who can and should make any adaptations necessary, so as to adjust it to their client's needs and capabilities (e.g., broaden the objectives in some of sessions so that their number is reduced). Thus, it can mean shortening the duration of a session, including or removing objectives, duplicating a session, adapting experiential activities to the client's age group and other characteristics, etc. The participant's age group should also be carefully considered during planning.

The proposal makes room for promoting requirements for social competence in all the sessions, starting with the first, though there might be greater emphasis in some rather than others. This does not mean the therapist needs to establish specific conditions for each of the clients during each session but that they must organize the proceedings in such a way as to include many of them simultaneously.

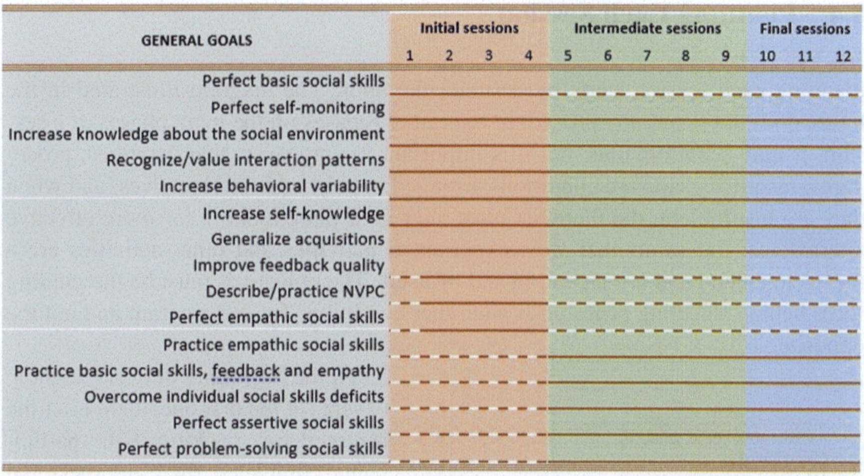

Fig. 8.5 Pacing objectives among initial, intermediary, and final sessions for a 12-session-long SST program

> These objectives are planned for all the participants, with greater or less emphasis, depending on the existing abilities and deficits or each group member.

The focus of the initial sessions should be on basic social skills (observing, describing, reporting, complimenting, asking and answering questions, and associating behavior with the conditions in which it occurred, considering that these behaviors are components of other skills and important for the other requisites for social competence). Social skills related to empathy and giving feedback are also the focus of initial sessions because, along with those basic ones for analyzing contingencies, they are requested by the therapist during the following sessions, as a support for learning other skills. It is worth remembering that generalization is also an important goal from the very first session and is initially promoted by assigning interpersonal homework.

When intermediary sessions begin, objectives related to each participant's specific deficits can start to be introduced. Considering that deficits in social skills related to assertiveness and empathy tend to occur more generally in the population, they were included as specific objectives in Table 8.1. In the next chapter, examples will be given for conducting two sessions focused on these skills.

During the final sessions, the objective to overcome participant's problems in terms of social skills and competence is maintained, albeit with a greater emphasis on values of coexistence. For this reason, the activities included work on thinking, reflecting, and analyzing interpersonal relationships in the participant's cultural context.

8.4 Planning Each Session

Planning each session starts by defining the aims. The diagram illustrated in the figure does not detail any procedure but rather focuses on the main phases of a session. It may seem obvious, but it is important to emphasize that activities, procedures, resources, etc., are conditions arranged to help achieve objectives, and when they are insufficient, the therapist must alter their plan, looking for more effective alternatives. Put in another way, experiential activities and other activities are a means to an end and not an end in and of itself. The objectives must be the guiding force behind selecting procedures and other conditions for the program and not the opposite.

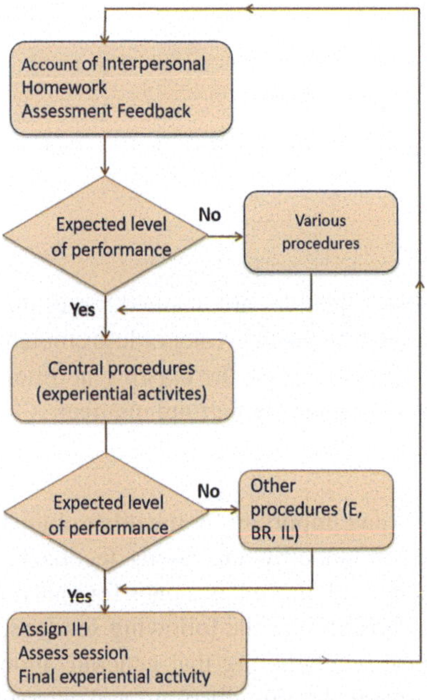

Fig. 8.6 Diagram of the steps of an SST session

At the beginning of every session, except for the first one, there is a time reserved for checking if the participants completed their interpersonal homework (IH) assigned in the previous session. Besides the various objectives related to IH practice (discussed in Chap. 6), this time enables the therapist to assess and promote the quality of the participants' account of their own behaviors and associated factors. This is a fundamental component of self-knowledge and is also important for identifying the social environment's rules (knowledge). In this initial phase, the therapist can conduct a brief experiential activity with the aim of preparing the participants for the session's objectives and activities (Fig. 8.6).

As seen in Table 8.2, if the participants have not shown the expected level of proficiency for the task, the therapist can proceed to use additional processes aiming to achieve it. If the difficulty persists, the therapist can (a) assign less complex tasks and (b) organize further training activities, especially through behavioral rehearsal. When the client has perfected the skills focused on by the IH, the therapist can then proceed to the central part of the session, which can also include further accounts, contingency analyses, and feedback.

The central part of the session is the longest and is dedicated to various activities, such as experiential activities and presentations or instructions (done in a dynamic and interactive way), exercises, analyzing excerpts from films, etc. They should be planned so as to contribute toward the goals specific to each session. When the participant shows satisfactory behavior, the therapist can start training new social skills, based on the portfolio. It may also be necessary, or not, depending on clients' behavior, to use other strategies at this moment, such as exercises (E), behavioral rehearsals (BR), and interactive instruction (II), before proceeding to the final part of the session. In some cases, it can be necessary to *recreate* one of the participants' everyday situations in order to access his/her behavior, paying attention to (a) his/her preexisting skills and psychological and social resources and difficulties and (b) reactions from people in the environment to his/her behavior while completing IH. In these cases, feedback, modeling, and shaping can be useful tools, and once improvements are apparent, so can assigning a task that requires behavior that is slightly similar to those the individual practiced.

The end of the session generally includes two activities: (a) assigning the next IH to be checked in the next session and (b) a brief assessment of the session. In this assessment, the therapist can ask for a group member to provide feedback to one member who participated more, on that occasion, in an experiential activity or exercise, or the therapist may also highlight the group's improvements that day. They can also do an experiential activity at the end, especially to encourage relaxation and group cohesion.

8.5 The Question of Generalization

Generalization of acquisitions must be planned and monitored from the beginning of the program. Planning generalization implies preparing for and including, right from the first sessions, procedures for ensuring or increasing the probability that new skills should be used in new environments or with different interlocutors. Thus, it is important to highlight encouragement of (a) behavioral variability, which helps to select and adjust behavior to different interactive demands, and (b) the client's sensitivity to environments' contingencies, associated to his/her contingency analysis in different situations (Fig. 8.7).

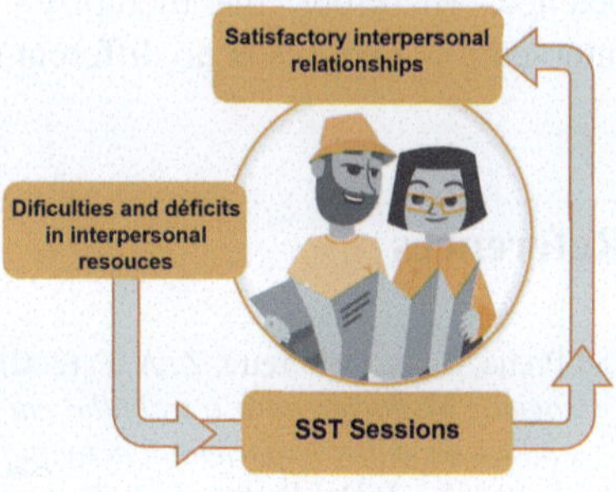

Fig. 8.7 Generalizations of learning

In SST programs, experiential activities, behavior analyses, behavioral rehearsals, and interpersonal homework are strategies favorable to the occurrence of generalization and should be used in this way. In any experiential activity, the therapist can adopt strategies to encourage the client to ask questions (a), (b), and (c).

8.6 From Planning to Conducting

The overall planning of the program and each session is the basis for a successful session. Thus, before effectively beginning a program, be it in group or individual format, the therapist can and should revise their plan. In order to do so, a checklist that includes the answers to the following items can be used, adaptable to group or individual interventions:

- *Did I evaluate my client(s) satisfactorily?*
- *Is the structure I have available favorable to conducting the intervention: physical environment, folder or box with texts and materials, minimal knowledge of clients that allows them to be grouped together?*
- *Have I organized the results of my assessments in a portfolio that details the clients' strengths and deficits?*
- *Have I defined objectives for each client, based on their preexisting skills and their deficits, as well as listed objectives that are common to the entire group?*

Once they have checked these items, the therapist may then begin conducting the program. The guidelines for this are given in the next chapter, but it is important to emphasize that besides following the script of the session, the therapist should pay attention to two aspects that are critical to the effectiveness of the intervention: on the one hand, the behaviors presented by the client, and on the other, to the opportunities that can arise or can be created to promote the requirements for social competence. Therefore, the therapist's actions are key to the effectiveness of any intervention, and this is no different for experiential activity SST programs.

References

Del Prette, A., & Del Prette, Z. A. P. (2001). *Psicologia das relações interpessoais e habilidades sociais: Vivências para o trabalho em grupo [The psychology of interpersonal relationships and social skills: Experiential activities for groups]* (1st ed.). Petrópolis, Brazil: Vozes.

Del Prette, A., & Del Prette, Z. A. P. (Orgs), (2017). *Habilidades Sociais: Intervenções efetivas em grupo [Social skills: Effective group interventions]* (3ird. ed.). São Paulo, Brazil: Casa do Psicólogo (3ª. ed.).

Del Prette, Z. A. P., & Del Prette, A. (1999). *Psicologia das Habilidades Sociais: Terapia, Educação e Trabalho [The psychology of social skills: Therapy, education and work]* (1st ed.). Petrópolis (SP), Brazil: Vozes.

Del Prette, Z. A. P., & Del Prette, A. (2005). *Psicologia das habilidades Sociais na Infância: Teoria e Prática [Psychology of social skills in childhood: Theory and practice]* (1st ed.). Petrópolis (SP), Brazil: Vozes.

Chapter 9
Conducting a Social Skills Program Oriented Toward Social Competence

Abstract In this chapter, specific guidelines are presented for conducting SST programs, considering the planning proposed in the previous chapter. Before focusing on conducting the sessions themselves, more detailed guidelines are given for conducting two kinds of activities that may be more difficult for the professional who is starting out in this area: experiential activities and interpersonal homework. To carry out the program sessions, a session planner that guides the therapist or facilitator's actions is suggested. Finally, a section on applying SST programs during individual intervention is presented. Group intervention and individual intervention are illustrated using case descriptions.

Keywords Experiential activities · Interpersonal homework · Sessions' plan model · Group social skills program · Individual social skills program

9.1 Conducting Experiential Activities

When structuring an experiential activity, the therapist or facilitator outlines a hypothetical scenario in which a participant taken from the Experiential Group (EG) will be asked to complete a task. For example, *We are in M's house, who is inviting ten people to meet up. Some already know each other and are talking. You arrive and realize that you do not know any of them. Your interpersonal task is to make contact and overcome isolation* (Fig. 9.1).

Fig. 9.1 A group of adolescents in Social Skills Training

Most experiential activities are structured as a problem for the client to solve by through their performance. In both group and individual SST, the therapist should support the participant's performance by enabling various attempts of practice, and providing positive reinforcement to his/her partial

Z. A. P. Del Prette, A. Del Prette, *Social Competence and Social Skills*,
https://doi.org/10.1007/978-3-030-70127-7_9

progress (modeling procedure). The facilitator should ask members belonging to the Observer Group (OG) to observe the behavior of those who are participating directly in the experiential activity, so that they may later describe their behavior and/or give feedback.

Sometimes, guided by observation and objectives, established previously or at the moment, the therapist can interrupt the experiential activity to:

- Positively reinforce certain behaviors (praise, brief comment, feedback)
- Recall norms pertaining to the experiential activity that may not have been considered by the participants
- Give specific instructions and in private to one or another member of the experiential activity (*whispering technique*)
- Restructure or change the situation, increasing or reducing the difficulty for one participant or another
- Ask an OG member for a description of the observed behaviors (Fig. 9.2)

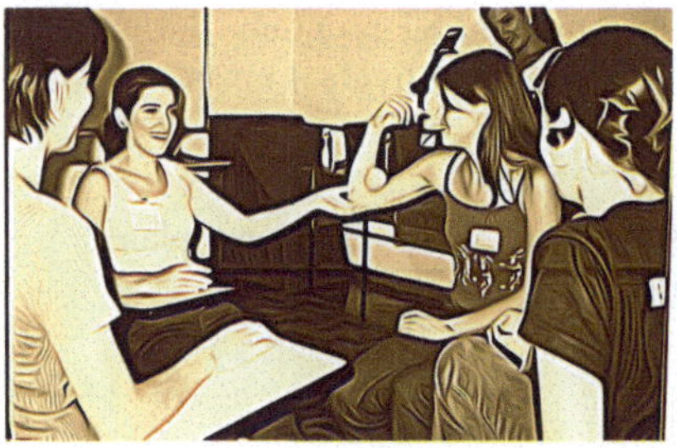

Fig. 9.2 Experiential activity for observation

The specific procedure for conducting each experiential activity is already described in each one of them (see Chap. 10). Even so, the therapist can make small changes in order to adjust elements of the situation to previously established goals, taking into account the client's existing skills and difficulties. For example, analogous experiential activities, which produce contingencies similar to those of daily life, can generate greater anxiety in some participants. In these cases, the therapist has the following alternatives:

- Include another participant as the focus of the practice, who would also benefit by participating in that specific situation
- Interrupt the experiential activity, allowing him/her to report the difficulty
- Reduce immediate requirements by increasing demand levels in small steps

In addition to these procedures, it is important to include participants with greater interpersonal difficulties only gradually. To do this, clients with generalized deficits in social skills, high anxiety, and history of little interpersonal success are initially requested only to collaborate in less difficult tasks, for example, in experiential activities whose focus is training others. For these cases, the therapist assigns homework with differentiated requirements. In all cases, it is important for the therapist to present positive feedback contingent to clients' behavior and ask other participants to practice giving this kind of support too. For those who have a better repertoire, the therapist can organize situations and demands, which require more elaborate behaviors, thus creating opportunity for others to learn by modeling.

9.2 Conducting Interpersonal Homework (IH)

Fig. 9.3 Conducting interpersonal homework in SST

The time set aside for reporting and analyzing IH requires specific procedures. It is recommended that the therapist starts off by asking a participant to recapitulate what was assigned. This already shows if the instruction given in the previous session was, in fact, correctly understood. Afterwards, the therapist can proceed with the following steps:

- Check, among those who did the task, who would like to start telling their experience.
- Positively reinforce the participant's account of their IH and behaviors according to the program's objectives, sometimes asking for feedback from another participant to the one who is reporting his/her experience.
- Provide specific guidelines or structure behavioral rehearsals in cases when a report shows behaviors occurring at levels lower than those expected but without giving any negative feedback.
- Check who did not perform the task and their reason for not doing it, writing down the explanation given, without any comment.

Checking IH can be time-consuming in the session. The therapist must be careful to balance this time with the other activities planned. When a participant is talking about the task, the facilitator should be aware of the following:

- Quality of the description the participant makes of their behaviors
- Context and immediate conditions, antecedent to behavior
- Consequences of behavior, immediate and probable in the medium and long term
- Anxiety and subjective response cost shown or reported by the client
- Social competence criteria met in the reported IH

In some cases, it may be necessary to structure a role-play in the session to simulate the described situation and to directly observe the participant's and the interlocutors' behaviors. This procedure is important for *calibrating* behavior and how it is reported, thus facilitating a more accurate assessment of how the IH was completed.

In the initial sessions, the therapist should accept reports of still incipient behaviors and gradually shape client's behavior to attain more elaborate forms of that behavior. The task should not be too demanding for the participant, which can be inferred by explanations such as: *I did actually do it, but it was difficult for me ...* Even in successful tasks, the response *cost* should be less than the results obtained. Thus, it is essential to order the tasks beginning with those most likely to have positive consequences. This procedure can avoid possible avoidance in the form of complaints, lack of opportunity, or even rationalization (see Chap. 6).

9.3 Organizing and Conducting the Program's Group Sessions

In this section, some suggestions are presented for organizing and conducting sessions of a preventative SST program for a group of adolescents of both sexes, aged 16–18 years. It should be noted here that:

- Each session's plan is a suggestion and should be adjusted to the participants' characteristics and needs.
- Planning each session is important for the success of the program, as well as the quality of how the therapist conducts it.
- A session plan (and also a program plan) can be changed according to new needs or insights the therapist might have while he/she is conducting it.
- In the presented plan, experiential activities are indicated in order to attain the stated objectives: they are also suggestions that the therapist will evaluate whether pertinent or not taking into account the clients' characteristics.

The plan for each session is presented below in a session planner, which contains (a) identification of session, with sequenced numbering, date, participants, and content to be addressed; (b) objectives, listing the social skills that will be promoted and identifying possible competing behaviors that should be addressed; (c) activities to be carried out, for example, name of experiential activity or exercise, topic of an interactive instruction (II), interpersonal homework to be assigned or analyzed, etc. At each session, the therapist should make notes about each participant's progress and any adjustments to be made in the following sessions. They can use the back of the booklet for this or some other way they find more practical for this ongoing and process evaluation.

To conduct the sessions, we chose to exemplify 7 out of a plan of 12 sessions, a number usually sufficient for a preventative SST program. These seven sessions include the first four, two intermediate, and one of the final ones. Depending on the application context and the participants' repertoire, some sessions can be broadened or reduced in their objectives, duration, and number. The experiential activities and exercises referred to in the sessions are described in detail in Chap. 10.

9.3.1 *Initial Sessions*

In group format, the initial sessions (defined as 1 to 4, according to Table 8.1 of the previous chapter) are important to encourage favorable process conditions, such as participants' engagement, revealing difficulties, mutual support, and group cohesion. Cohesion occurs mainly when the therapist (a) preferentially resorts to positive feedback among the participants, (b) assigns generic IH in the first sessions, and (c) requests an evaluation of the session.

In terms of acquisition process, these sessions should encourage (a) basic social skills, including giving positive feedback; (b) discrimination of demands and analysis of contingencies, associated with knowledge and self-knowledge (still in the process of probing); (c) decoding and refining nonverbal and paralinguistic components (NVPC); and (d) empathic social skills. At this stage, generic interpersonal tasks are recommended (for all), aimed at *leveling* the participants' repertoire in the aforementioned objectives.

A suggestion for planning and conducting four initial sessions that keep these objectives in mind is presented next. For each of them, a brief description is made with additional clarifications to those summarized in the session planner (Table 9.1).

Table 9.1 Organizing SST program: Session 1 model

SESSION NO. 1 Date: ____/____/____ **Participants:** ____________________ **CONTENT:** Initial contact; information about the program; basic social skills (observing, describing, praising, thanking compliments, initial self-knowledge).	
Objectives	**Activities**
Getting to know the other participants of the group	EA: *Name tags*
Learning about the program	II: Presentation of the program
Praise and thank compliments Recognize relevant praises	EA: *Praising is good and I like it*
Observe/describe/report Relate behaviors to demands	EA: *Observing* II: *Self-monitoring*
Increase Self-Knowledge	EA: *Self-evaluation* OR EA: *Self-knowledge*
Understanding the importance of IH Praise (and other objectives common to all IHs, Chapter 6)	II: Importance and functioning of IH IH-1 Assignment: Praise the behavior of a relative
Evaluate the session on a descriptive basis	Conduct session evaluation
Ease any tensions in the session	EA: *Dancing to the tune*

Abbreviations: EA, Experiential Activity; II, Interactive Instruction; IH, Interpersonal Homework.

In group programs, the initial session is the first moment of contact and interaction between some of the participants. Therefore, we suggest starting off with each one introducing themselves, including additional information, such as how they spend their free time, etc. This activity can also be done as an experiential activity, such as the *Name Tags* activity, in which each person introduces him/herself, including information about leisure, hobbies, etc., for example.

Afterwards, the therapist should make a brief II about how the program works, why the classroom layout has been arranged in a semicircle, and the objectives of the program and the session. This is also the time to answer any questions about the program.

The suggested experiential activities and interactive instructions and discussions initially aim to encourage self-knowledge and self-monitoring, observation, identification, and analysis of manifest (observable) behaviors, as well as the inference of covert thoughts, beliefs, self-corrections, feelings, self-observation, and descriptive reporting of behaviors. During experiential activities, the therapist should mediate the interactions so that some participants' reports are not criticized by a colleague, valuing objective descriptions, based on facts rather than inferences (Table 9.2).

Table 9.2 Organizing SST program: Session 2 model

SESSION NO. 2 Date: ____/____/____ **Participants:** ____________________ **CONTENT:** Social communication skills, feedback, self-control, analyzing interactions, making friends, discriminating and sharing personal information spontaneously, increasing knowledge and self-knowledge	
Objectives	**Activities**
Praise family member's behaviors (and objectives common to all IHs, Chapter 6)	Analysis of IH-1
Evaluate personal anxiety and increase self-knowledge	EA: *The Silence Game*
Identify communication Social Skill (SS) Identify the characteristics of good feedback/feedback's characteristics	II: Communication and Feedback
Improve feedback	E: Practicing feedback
Initiate and maintain conversation, ask relevant questions, share information freely, respond to spontaneously shared personal information	EA. *Making friends*
Improve self-control over behavior (and objectives common to all IHs, Chapter 6)	II: Self-control and Social Competence IH-2 Assignment: Leave a little of what you are drinking in the glass (water, soda). IH-3 Assignment: Give Positive Feedback to a colleague´s or family member´s behavior
Evaluate the session on a descriptive basis Give feedback to classmates	Conduct and evaluate the session
Deal with stress and relax	EA: *Dealing with worries and stress*

Abbreviations: EA, Experiential Activity; E. Exercise; II, Interactive Instruction; IH, Interpersonal Homework.

Another objective, which appears from the beginning of the initial sessions, is to generalize acquisitions, as already mentioned. This is done through IH. In the first session, the therapist briefly (II) explains its importance: (a) to consolidate skills learned in the session; (b) as a privileged condition of observation and self-observation, complemented by the report in the following session; and (c) in the participant's evaluation of the lessons learned. In order to articulate IH with the objectives and behaviors in the session, this task is assigned to occur in the family context, for example, *Praise the behavior of a family member*.

At the end, the therapist asks for an evaluation of the session, which creates a demand for checking and modeling descriptive reports, for example, rather than *I enjoyed it, it was cool!*, the therapist asks the participants to specify what was good and why they enjoyed it. The final moment is also important to ensure that everyone is alright. The first session is of expectation and fears, so it should be finished with a playful and relaxing activity. We suggest the experiential activity called *Dancing to the tune.*

In the second session, the therapist begins by checking the IH, assigned in the previous session. As mentioned above, in addition to the various IH objectives (Chap. 6), this analysis allows the therapist to evaluate and adjust the quality of the participant's report on their own behaviors and associated variables, which contributes to their self-knowledge, as well as to how well they identify rules and norms in their social environment. (If necessary, review previous section of this chapter, Conducting Interpersonal Homework.)

Afterwards, the therapist conducts the experiential activity *The silence game*. In general, this experience reproduces a situation in which the participant finds it difficult to discriminate what is expected of him/her, creating an opportunity for them to develop self-knowledge of their abilities when faced with this type of demand. In this experiential activity, the therapist must be careful to help participants feel like they belong to the Experiential Group (EG) dealing with their anxiety, should they need it. When analyzing the activity after it is concluded, the therapist checks the level of anxiety asking participants to rate it on a scale from 1 to 5. They discuss how each one dealt with the situation and if the participants identified which factors of the situation were causing the anxiety. The experiential activity can be repeated with some members of the OG, in which case less anxiety is expected. The comparison between the two anxiety ratings provides insights into explaining this change.

The therapist uses some of the behaviors observed in this experiential activity as initial examples for the interactive instruction on *Communication and Feedback*. He/she then uses visual support resources to emphasize, briefly and objectively, the characteristics of good feedback. For example, based on the text on the topic (Chap. 6), they might use a PowerPoint presentation, followed by the E: Practicing feedback, which should be exercised in the context of the session.

Still in the context of communication skills, the therapist conducts the experiential activity *Making friends*, which also includes training in discrimination in social interaction (especially in terms of spontaneously shared personal information and timing). Afterwards, the therapist concludes this experiential activity by giving feedback, guiding the participants so they may practice among themselves, even at moments outside the session, based on what was seen during the experiential activity.

The therapist then gives a brief account of what is self-control and the importance of it (see Chap. 2), assigning two homework tasks. The first is not exactly an interpersonal task. The objective, in the same way, is that the participants notice the difficulty of changing automatic patterns of behaviors in apparently simple tasks. The second objective is to practice giving feedback outside the session.

Finally, after evaluating the session, the experiential activity *Dealing with worry and stress*, which articulates aspects of self-knowledge and body/facial expression, is suggested (Table 9.3).

Table 9.3 Organizing SST program: Session 3 model

SESSION NO. 3 Date: ____/____/____ **Participants**: ____________________ **CONTENT**: Non-verbal and Paralinguistic Components (NVPC) and making friends	
Objectives	**Activities**
Practicing giving positive feedback (and common objectives to all IHs, Chapter. 6)	Analysis of IH-2 and IH-3 II: Mnemonics for IH
Maintain eye contact	EA: *Eye Contact*
Understand the role played by/importance of NVPC	II: NVPC
Practicing and decoding NVPC	EA: *Talking without speaking*
Listen attentively and make friends	EA: *What my friend told me*
Monitor NVPC Observe the impact of one's behavior on others (and objectives common to all IHs, Chapter 6)	IH-4 Assignment: Talking with an acquaintance or family member, alternating NVPC and checking impact on the interaction.
Evaluate the session on a descriptive basis Give feedback to classmates	Conduct session evaluation
Developing affection within the group	EA: *Bonding with your group*

Abbreviations: EA, Experiential Activity; II, Interactive Instruction; IH, Interpersonal Homework; Non-verbal and Paralinguistic Components (NVPC).

> NVPC should be targeted throughout the program.

The session begins by reporting and analyzing IH. After the task reports, the therapist begins the first experiential activity *Eye contact* that is related to the main topic and serves as a *warm-up*. Then, a brief presentation of the NVPC can be given based on the content presented at the end of Chap. 2 and other references, (e.g., Del Prette & Del Prette, 1999, 2009), emphasizing what is culturally expected. Emphasize that markedly different cultural practices may hinder the acceptance of the individual in another group. On the other hand, it explains how the understanding of these practices can contribute to social competence. The two experiential activities – *Talking without speaking* and *What my friend told me* – create the conditions for the analysis and an initial improvement of the verbal and nonverbal expressiveness of the participants.

The IH assigned (*talking with an acquaintance or family member, alternating NVPC, and checking impact on the interaction*) analyzes the importance of NVPC, especially when they are deficient. After evaluating the session, the final experiential activity (*Bonding with the Group*) should keep the participants' focus on conditions of closeness and cohesion (Table 9.4).

Table 9.4 Organizing SST program: Session 4 model

SESSION NO. 4 Date: ____/____/____ Participants: ____________________ CONTENT: Empathy and its components	
Objectives	**Activities**
Practice variability in the NVCPs (and common objectives to everyone in the IH - Chap. 6)	Analysis of IH-4
Assume the other's perspective	EA: *In someone else's shoes*
Understand the meaning of empathy Identify behavioral, affective and cognitive characteristics Discriminate and practice NVPCs of empathy Develop values associated with empathy	II: Empathy and empathic SS E: *Opting for empathy*
Evaluate the session on a descriptive basis Give feedback to classmates	Conduct session evaluation
Demonstrate empathy and analyze behavior (and objectives common to all IHs, see Chapter 6)	Assignment IH-5: Demonstrate empathy to a friend or a family member
Raise awareness of values of coexistence	EA: *Doing good is good*

Abbreviations: EA, Experiential Activity; E, Exercise; II, Interactive Instruction; IH, Interpersonal Homework

After analyzing IH-4, the therapist begins the experiential activity *In someone else's shoes* (Chap. 10). Then, he/she initiates the II, asking them to describe what happened, the NVPC that they observed in the experiential activity, and what importance they evaluated to *Assume the other's perspective*. He/she explains the meaning of this expression as a component of the social skills class called empathy, differentiating empathy, pro-empathy, and pseudo-empathy. We suggest using audiovisual material, excerpts from movies, cartoons, news, etc., as well as instructional material on the subject (see also Del Prette & Del Prette, 2001, 2005). There is a reasonable amount of material available on empathy, including research showing its occurrence also in animals of different species such as chimpanzees, elephants, dogs, and others. The objective, in this case, should be not only the understanding but also the awareness of values of coexistence guided by the notion of empathy.

Next, the facilitator conducts the E, *Opting for empathy*, arranging the participants in pairs. He/she draws attention to the effects this skill can have and makes explicit that the expression of empathy can help solve interpersonal difficulties. He/she concludes by referring to the importance of also expressing empathy when positive events occur to people (around them).

At the end, the therapist assigns the IH of the week about expressing empathy and conducts the session evaluation. He/she can end the session with the experiential activity *Doing good is good*.

9.3.2 Intermediate Sessions

The intermediate sessions of the program (5 to 9, according to the general scheme set out in the previous chapter) aim to address each participant's specific difficulties in terms of social competence requirements. If the first sessions were successful, the therapist can already count on everyone's basic social skills as factors that already naturally lead to the broadening of each member's repertoire, supporting their more intentional work with the group. However, it is up to the therapist to mediate this *collaboration* by involving all the participants, now with an emphasis on overcoming each other's deficits and promoting the requirements of social competence.

Generally, most participant's that seek professional help from a psychologist have deficits in empathy and basic skills already covered in previous sessions, as well as in assertive skills and problem-solving, which is why session plans 6 and 8 focus on these two classes, respectively. The other sessions of this intermediate phase could focus on other group difficulties or expand subclasses of assertiveness and empathy (Table 9.5).

Table 9.5 Organizing SST program: Session 6 model

SESSION NO. 6 Date: ____/____/____ **Participants:** ____________________ **CONTENT:** Assertiveness and its subclasses	
Objectives	**Activities**
(IH objectives from previous session)	Analysis of previous week's IH
Recognize the relationship between rights, responsibilities and assertiveness	EA: *Rights and obligations*
Identify characteristics of assertive SS Recognize different classes of assertive SS Differentiate assertive, non-assertive, aggressive Recognize the risks and challenges of assertiveness	II: Assertiveness
Recognize passive and aggressive responses Practice assertive alternatives	E: Practicing assertive responses
Deal with criticism (and objectives common to all IHs, see Chapter 6)	IH Assignment: When criticized, choose among the alternatives: (a) to accept if pertinent; (b) partially reject; (c) totally reject.
Reflect on the importance of assertiveness	II: Conduct excerpt analysis of a movie about assertiveness
Demonstrate positive affect as a complement to assertiveness	EA: *Expressing affection*

Abbreviations: EA, Experiential Activity; E, Exercise; II Interactive Instruction; IH, Interpersonal Homework

The therapist begins the session by asking the participants to report on how their IH, assigned in the previous session, went. He/she can then use the experiential activity *Rights and obligations* followed by establishing relations between the behaviors observed/required in the experiential activity and the topic of the session. With the support of teaching resources (slides, excerpts from movies for analysis, and images), he/she gives a brief description of the classes and subclasses of assertive SS. The therapist continues with the exercise of analyzing, choosing, and developing assertive alternatives of *Practicing assertive responses*. In some cases, assertive behaviors should be preceded by an expression of empathy. Thus, we suggest using the experiential activity called *Expressing affection* as the next step in the session, creating an opportunity for the therapist to emphasize the importance of associating these two classes of social skills. He/she assigns the IH of the week, focusing on assertiveness.

The therapist could present an excerpt from a movie that deals with assertiveness (e.g., *Amanhã Nunca Mais* – a Brazilian movie), asking participants to apply what they have learned by analyzing the character's behaviors. In this case, he/she can end with the session evaluation (Table 9.6).

Table 9.6 Organizing SST program: Session 8 model

SESSION NO. 8 Date: ____/____/____ **Participants:** ________________________	
CONTENT: Problem solving and decision making	
Objectives	**Activities**
(IH objectives from previous session)	Analysis of previous week's IH.
Come up with alternative response to a problem situation	EA: *Watch where you step*
Understand the rationale of the problem-solving process and the steps needed for it.	II: Solving problems and taking decisions
Practice the steps for problem solving and decision making in group settings.	EA: *Solving interpersonal problems*
Evaluate the session on a descriptive basis Give feedback to colleagues	Conduct session evaluation
Solve problems, evaluate problem solving alternatives (and objectives common to all IHs, see Chapter 6)	IH Assignment: Choose a problem situation in one's own life, develop two alternatives, test them and evaluate the differences in effectiveness.
Reflect on behavioral alternatives	EA: *Never the same*

Abbreviations: EA, Experiential Activity; II Interactive Instruction; IH, Interpersonal Homework

Conducting this session is not different from leading the others. It is expected that the reader has already become familiar with the basics of following these steps. It is important to highlight that the problem-solving process was studied in psychology, and there are proposals for analysis and putting solutions into practice, tested in controlled situations. During this activity, the process is carried out as a group, establishing demands for group coordination. For learning purposes, practicing a potentially effective process is more important than the final result achieved by the group. This should be the focus of the therapist's attention.

9.3.3 *Final Sessions*

In the final sessions (10 to 12), the learning of social competence requirements must be quite consolidated, as should be the practice of empathetic and assertive skills, and a greater group readiness in basic social skills should be perceptible and actively supporting the intervention process. Therefore, this is a particularly good time for reflection on the values of coexistence and for improving knowledge about cultural norms for social life. At this stage, more time and better conditions can be expected/planned, in each session, for reports on generalization and the impact of new interactions and behaviors in the natural context (Table 9.7).

Table 9.7 Organizing SST program: Session 11 model

SESSION NO. 11 **Date**: ___/___/___ **Participants**: __________ **CONTENT:** Values of coexistence	
Objectives	**Activities**
(IH objectives from previous session)	Analysis of previous week's IH
Identify value and interactions mediated by values	EA: *Social interaction values*
Recognize perceptual biases and prejudice Analyze the impact of prejudice on social interactions Identify alternatives to limit or reduce bias.	EA: *Let's get to know* Peter (if children or parents) OR EA: *Joana* 's story (if teenagers and adults)
To value cooperation and teamwork Reflect on values of coexistence	V: *What can we learn from geese?*
Identify cooperative interactions, give positive feedback, cooperate when faced with a demand for it (and objectives common to all IHs, see Chapter 6).	IH - Give positive feedback to a person who demonstrated cooperation IH - Cooperate with a stranger
Evaluate the session on a descriptive basis Give feedback to classmates	Conduct session evaluation
Raise awareness of values of coexistence	MR: Watch message involving values of coexistence (*Gentileza gera gentileza*)

Abbreviations: EA, Experiential Activity; E, Exercise; IH, Interpersonal Homework; MR, Media Resource (Short advertisement available on YouTube at: https://www.youtube.com/watch?v=nexOPbgQkHk)

This session includes reflective questions that address behavioral problems related to prejudice and judgment. The previous week's IH accounts can be used to introduce the theme. Then, the therapist conducts the experiential activity *Social interaction values* that should prepare the group for *Joana's story*. This is a longer experiential activity that articulates much of the previous learning, such as group coordination, interaction analysis, feedback, exposition, etc. For groups of children, or parents, the *Let's get to know* Peter version can be used. These two alternatives of experiential activities take a long time and lead to an interesting reflection on prejudice. As idealized, the program described here refers to a preventative SST. In this case, the therapist can broaden the discussion by bringing research data about factors that are at the root of prejudice.

At the end, the assigned IH also involves valuing and demonstrating cooperation. After the session evaluation, the therapist can end with a video that raises awareness, e.g., *The virus of kindness* (https://www.youtube.com/watch?v=WL_UK2DTTG4, accessed on 27/11/18), or some music suggestive of cooperation.

This was the last session described as part of a suggestion for preventative SST, intended for teenagers of both sexes, aged 16–18 years. Of course, this content represents a shortened sample of SST sessions, and depending on the characteristics and needs of the participants, the program may include several more. Between a detailed descriptive report and very general guidelines, we decided to select what is important for the reader interested in this type of intervention.

9.3.4 *Illustrative Case of SST in Group Format*

SST programs, in group or individual format, are usually reported in articles in journals and periodicals (e.g., http://www.rihs.ufscar.br/artigos-em-periodicos) and as book chapters (see Del Prette & Del Prette, 2017), emphasizing the results rather than descriptions of cases. To illustrate, an example of intervention in group format focusing on one participant is described next. This may help understand the process better for those beginning to conduct SST programs. The intervention was done with Janet (fictitious name) who participated in an SST group conducted by the authors.

Background and Complaints

Janet was 21 years old. She was doing a secretarial course in the evenings and lived with her parents, two older brothers (23 and 25 years old), and a younger sister aged 7. Her father worked as a bricklayer, while her mother, with Janet's help, did the household chores. The two brothers also worked as bricklayers. Their house was made of bricks. It had three bedrooms, a living room, and a kitchen. Janet complained about conflicts with her brothers who, when their father was not there, decided what she could and could not choose regarding the clothes she wore, her friendships (just with girls), and places to go. In addition, they required more effort from her in relation to household chores to do, such as cleaning, ironing, preparing food, etc. Her father was severe, and, most of the time, he supported his sons. Janet was unhappy and said she did not know what to do.

Starting the SST

Janet applied for the SST, for girls aged between 17 and 22, through an institution that supports young people with low incomes. According to the initial interview and observation, Janet had some difficulties, such as (a) not much eye contact; (b) deficits in social contacts and conversational and friend-making social skills (recounting episodes, telling stories, engaging in jokes, etc.); (c) moaning tone of voice; and (d) frustrated attempts to confront the authoritarianism of her father and siblings. Discreet support from her mother, the initiative to look for a job, and enrolling on a secretarial course could be included in the list of existing personal skills and environmental resources.

Janet's participation in the SST group was discreet, and she rarely took the initiative to talk to her classmates. The first interpersonal homework assignments, as told by Janet, showed evidence of an attempt at avoidance, claiming a lack of opportunity or complaining about some physical problem (headache) or domestic arguments.

Progress in SST

Without expecting Janet to volunteer to participate in the experiential activities, the therapist gave her less demanding tasks to do with some classmates from the group the first few times. The first couple of times she participated actively, the therapist praised her efforts. In addition, Janet was chosen to participate in the experiential activity, *Feedback: How and when* (Del Prette & Del Prette, 2001, p. 134), receiving positive feedback from some classmates. After that, she was interested in taking part in new experiential activities. At the end of the session, she was assigned the interpersonal homework: *Ask any question to a classmate in your course, preferably someone with whom you have not yet spoken with*. She was also asked to look at her interlocutor when asking the question. When the tasks were discussed in another session, someone noticed that *she was looking at people*. In fact, eye contact had already been established through instruction and positive consequences in the sessions. As Janet progressed in making eye contact, the instruction *look into their eyes* was no longer given. In the following session, Janet was pleased to have done the task and started learning contingency analysis, describing her behavior and that of the interlocutor. As for the *moaning* tone of voice, a classmate with adequate verbal articulation collaborated as a model in a role-play about interactions with family members in which this type of speech was more accentuated. Janet changed the type of speech also by understanding that she had to face situations *without this type of strategy*. The therapist then made an effort to teach Janet and other participants to carry out contingency analysis, asking them to participate in new experiential activities, in which basic social skills (describing behavior, asking questions, responding to questions, etc.) were also improved. Janet asked to learn to deal with family members, which was the aim of most of the young women (in the program). It was at this stage that the therapist explained the importance of the *win-win* concept, introducing appropriate experiential activities for interactions with reciprocal gains. Moreover, homework was given involving positive reciprocity in negotiating with her parents about choosing her own clothes and friends to study with and go out with.

Some Results
In short, Janet learned a set of new social skills, the consequences of which were positive, because she was trained (especially by shaping and modeling) to *teach* people in their social environment to observe her behaviors and react to them positively. She also changed her style of speech, greatly improved eye contact, and no longer talked about unhappiness. She became more popular in the group and was often praised by classmates. One week before the sessions finished, Janet reported that she had got a job in a department store, which motivated the group to celebrate by having a little party.

9.4 Organizing and Conducting SST in Individual Intervention

In the context of individualized clinical care, the procedures for planning evaluation (interviews, observation, using inventories) and intervention (shaping, modeling, instruction, role-plays, behavioral rehearsal, and homework) for SST are similar to the group processes (see Kelly, 2002). Acquiring new social skills as well as improving those already possessed by the client and decreasing concurrent behaviors will also involve learning processes such as instruction, shaping, and modeling. These processes should be encouraged in close articulation with practice, both within and outside the session. Despite some similarities with group intervention, individual intervention requires some adaptations, particularly in the case of experiential activities.

As in group SST, the therapist's access to the client's behavior is also important in individual intervention. Three techniques for this should be mentioned, which are role-playing, behavioral rehearsals, and experiential activities. Considering intervention with children, sometimes the experiential activities also allow access to parents' behavior, when there is an opportunity for them to participate.

9.4.1 How to Use Experiential Activities in Individual Intervention

Some adaptations may be necessary concerning experiential activities and exercises, produced for group work. Among those presented in Chap. 10, some are more easily adapted to individual intervention.

By adapting the experiential activities, the therapist can assume different roles when dialogue is used to work with the client. For example, the *Making friends* experiential activity (Chap. 10) can be conducted with the therapist acting as the client's interlocutor, using the questions suggested for the experiential activity and helping the client to provide, discriminate, and use personal information spontaneously shared in the interaction. In the experiential activities that contain texts for analysis and reflection, the therapist can give the text to the client and discuss the content in the next session. The exercises which entail analyzing interactions and coming up with alternatives of social skills, such as the *Opting for empathy and the Practicing assertive responses* exercises, can be carried out in the session, in the case of teenagers and adults, where the therapist chooses the items which are most relevant to the client's difficulties.

In intervention with children (see the example at the end of the chapter), the therapist can, when possible, ask the mother, sibling, and some friends to take part in some of the games and experiential activities. For example, in the experiential activity *Hot and Cold*, an object was hidden somewhere in the house (kitchen, bedroom) in which the child refused to go into alone. In this case, first a friend went into the room and, after receiving *tips* of *Hot and Cold*, found the object. The others clapped or praised them for their behavior. After being exposed to the *model*, the client was also asked to find another object hidden in that room. The therapist stood at a distance, saying *Hot* or *Cold*, without getting near the place. When they had completed the task, following the model provided by the friend, the client was also positively reinforced. No comment (e.g., *Before you didn't go in there alone*) was made. In this experiential activity, family members were instructed to observe how the therapist behaved.

9.4.2 Using Other Techniques, Procedures, and Resources

Role-play procedures can be used as a way of accessing the client's behavior in the context or after an experiential activity. This makes it easier for the therapist (a) to access the client's behavior in interaction, comparing them with their reports; (b) to help the client with self-observation and adjusting their reports (description of what they did and how they did it) more closely to their observed behaviors; and (c) to model the client's account and analysis of the contingencies in the interactions. Considering the interlocution restricted to the therapist, the therapist can take on roles and also adopt characters suited to the moment, such as the client's boss, friend, father, teacher, etc.

Another technique that the therapist can use to a great extent is behavioral rehearsals (see Chap. 6), aimed at honing the client's target behaviors, practiced in sessions and shaped by the contingencies arranged by the therapist. This technique is important for shaping the client's behavior toward their goals for learning social skills relevant tasks to their daily lives.

It is recommended that the therapist should pay special attention to interpersonal homework assignments. In individual intervention, they are often recounted only to the therapist but may have some of the functions that were provided for group programs, as explained in previous chapters. When it comes to child intervention, interpersonal homework can be assigned to the child and their parents (mother most of the time). During or following the reporting and feedback of these tasks, the therapist may conduct a discussion and eventually conduct a behavioral rehearsal in order to (a) correct some aspects of the client's behavior, e.g., eye contact; (b) encourage a more accurate report of his/her behavior; and (c) introduce another participant in a symbolic way (e.g., repeat this as if your mother was present).

Instructional activities, especially interactive instruction, can be part of individual intervention, but in a more restricted way, in the form of a conversation. In this case, reading suggestions regarding social skills as well as a brief explanation of concepts may be useful for different types of clientele. In child intervention, the therapist can recommend texts or resources (educational movies, games, booklets) to parents or teachers and other people important in the child's life (e.g., activity books and games, texts, movies, etc.). In interventions with adolescents or adults, recommending books is also an option to be considered.

Multimedia resources, especially short movie clips and videos, should be considered as useful material for discussion and orientation in the sessions. This often allows the therapist to check client beliefs and values about characters and how closely their own behavior resembles or differs from their character's behavior. In some cases, especially with adolescents and adults, some movies can be recommended for them to watch at home. Some excerpts from movies can be used as (a) modeling behavior soon to be practiced in a session; (b) analyzing inadequate behavior when training discrimination of demands, situations, social norms, etc.; and (c) reflecting on values of coexistence and criteria of the ethical dimension/ethical criteria.

9.4.3 Illustrative Case of SST in Individual Format

With children, using SST may eventually include interlocutors in order to facilitate procedures involving interaction. To do this, classmates and family are invited both to the clinic and institution, for example, school, to take part in some sessions. As an example, child intervention is briefly described next (Del Prette, 2012).

Background and Complaints
An 8-year-old girl was brought by her mother to the psychologist's clinic. The mother's main complaint was that her daughter *had visions of her grandmother*, who had died a few months ago. The mother also said that the child (a) refused to go into places (rooms) in the house without someone else, because she feared the presence of her grandmother; (b) she talked about this topic nonstop; (c) she avoided contact with her classmates; and (d) she fought with an older brother who mocked her. The director of the school reported that the child had bad grades and was mostly isolated.

Intervention
In addition to the two sessions devoted to evaluation with the family and the child herself, two more sessions were held at school, mainly focusing on the friendship between grandparents and grandchildren. In addition, four sessions took place at the child's home with the participation of some of her friends, invited by the client, performing one of the tasks assigned to her by the therapist. Desensitization, model-

ing, shaping, and instructional procedures were used in association with games, such as the experiential activity: *Hot and Cold* (Chap. 10). In addition to providing some guidelines to the parents, her brother was instructed to stop mocking her.

Obtained Results
School and parental reports indicated a decrease and subsequent suppression of verbalizations about fearing possible appearances of the grandmother's spirit. In addition, the child started to use the spaces previously avoided. At school, she got better grades and started having more contact with friends and classmates again, having them over as a group at her home for various activities.

Follow-Up
After 2 months, the therapist followed up with the family (mother and brother) and had a brief interview with the child and teacher. The informants reported maintenance of the gains brought about by the intervention. In addition, contact with the child showed evidence of new gains, for instance, (a) better verbal fluency, (b) accounts of playing at school, and (c) reports of improvements in learning at school.

Additional Observations
This case is quite suggestive of the use of SST as a main intervention strategy (see Chap. 5). Learning new social skills increased contact with schoolmates, diversifying the subjects of conversation and playing with other children. Concurrent behaviors such as talking about her *grandmother's death* or *apparition* decreased, as the attention of family and teachers was directed to skills such as talking about schoolwork and reports of encounters and games with friends. Attention also ceased to occur as consequence of the behaviors of (a) requiring the presence of someone to go into an isolated environment, (b) provoking the sibling, and (c) avoiding classmates.

9.5 Therapist's Final Analysis

At the end of a session, the therapist has not yet finished their work. Rather, each session always provides new elements for analysis and decisions about the program as a whole and in particular about the next session. Writing down a summary of the session, including meaningful gains of each participant and any new deficits identified, may mean changing the next session and even restructuring the program.

An important analysis for the therapist to make is about how he/she conducted his/her own session. Here, some questions would be appropriate and certainly the most important of them is: *Am I able to encourage the relevant gains and in different ways according to the participants' needs?* The answer to this question cannot be based on an overall impression but on the behavior of each participant. It can lead to other questions such as:

- *Am I being clear enough in my explanations?*
- *Am I identifying new difficulties for each of the participants?*

- *Am I distributing my attention in a reasonably balanced way among the participants?*
- *Are there any indicators of a supportive relationship between the participants?*
- *Are there any indicators of therapeutic alliance with the group and with each of the participants?*
- *Are there any indicators of generalization of gains outside the sessions?*
- *Are there any indicators that the gains are relevant to the social tasks of each participant?*

These reflections are important and are part of the process analysis that should lead to the desired end results. To do this, after summarizing the session and answering these questions, the therapist can (a) record important reminders for the next session; (b) define personalized homework for different participants; and (c) jot down topics or facts to address in the next session.

In terms of achieving the objectives, it is not enough just to consider spontaneous reports such as *I'm really enjoying participating.* It is essential to check whether the goals are being successfully converted into the expected gains throughout the sessions and whether the established conditions, especially those brought about by the therapist's practice, are sufficient and related to these results.

References

Del Prette, A. (2012). Atendimento a uma criança que relatava ver o espírito da avó: Um estudo de caso [Therapy for a child who reported having seen her grandmother's ghost], *Estudos de Psicologia* (Campinas, SP), *29*(2), 285–292.

Del Prette, A., & Del Prette, Z. A. P. (2001). *Psicologia das relações interpessoais e habilidades sociais: Vivências para o trabalho em grupo [The psychology of interpersonal relationships and social skills: Experiential activities for groups]* (1st ed.). Petrópolis, Brazil: Vozes.

Del Prette, A., & Del Prette, Z. A. P. (2009). Componentes não verbais e paralinguísticos das habilidades sociais [Nonverbal and paralinguistic components of social skills]. In: A. Del Prette, & Z. A. P. Del Prette (Orgs.), *Psicologia das habilidades sociais: Diversidade teórica e suas implicações [The psychology of social skills: Theoretical diversity and its implications]* (pp. 147–186). Petrópolis, Brazil: Vozes.

Del Prette, A., & Del Prette, Z. A. P. (Orgs.). (2017). *Habilidades Sociais: Intervenções efetivas em grupo [Social skills: Effective group interventions]* (3rd ed.). São Paulo, Brazil: Casa do Psicólogo.

Del Prette, Z. A. P., & Del Prette, A. (1999). *Psicologia das Habilidades Sociais: Terapia, Educação e Trabalho [The psychology of social skills: Therapy, education and work]* (1st ed.). Petrópolis, Brazil: Vozes.

Del Prette, Z. A. P., & Del Prette, A. (2005). *Psicologia das habilidades Sociais na Infância: Teoria e Prática [Psychology of social skills in childhood: Theory and practice]* (1st ed.). Petrópolis, Brazil: Vozes.

Kelly, J. (2002). A Entrenamiento de las Habilidades Sociales [Social Skills Training] (8a. ed.). Bilbao: Desclee de Brouwer.

Chapter 10
Experiential Activities and Other Procedures and Techniques for Social Skills Programs

Abstract This chapter includes 25 experiential activities and two practical exercises, tested for SST programs and referred to in the files presented in the previous chapter. They are grouped into sets of (1) experiential activities for beginning and ending a session; (2) experiential activities used for the main part of the session, aimed at developing and practicing skills; and (3) other exercises for analyzing and practicing skills.

Keywords Social Skills Training · Experiential activities · Group interventions

All the activities presented in this chapter should be selected according to the objectives of the program. They can also be used in other educational processes in school contexts, work, health, etc. Throughout the descriptions of each experiential activity, the term facilitator[1] was adopted as a reference to the professional who is conducting the activity. This professional should preferably be from the area of psychology but may be from related areas provided that they are properly trained to conduct these programs.

10.1 Experiential Activities for the Beginning and End of a Session

10.1.1 Name Tags

At the beginning of the session, the facilitator gives each participant a name tag with blanks to fill out, as shown below. He/she asks them to write their name (not their surname) clearly in capital letters and to walk around the room observing the others and their names. The facilitator then asks each one to exchange their name tag with

[1] In this chapter, the words facilitator and therapist are used interchangeably.

Z. A. P. Del Prette, A. Del Prette, *Social Competence and Social Skills*,
https://doi.org/10.1007/978-3-030-70127-7_10

someone else, with whom they have had little contact. They should then fill in the *Hobby* (a) gap, imagining what hobby this person could have. The facilitator asks everyone to walk a bit more and exchange name tags again, without getting their own. The participants should now fill in the *Skill* (a) gap of the person's name tag. Afterwards, everyone should look for their own tag and write *R for right* or *W for wrong* considering their classmates' assumptions. They should fill in the correct information in gap (b) for the wrong assumptions. Finally, the facilitator asks them to find the classmates who filled in their tag, congratulating them on the right answers and talking about movies and favorite food, as well as completing these items on the tag (Fig. 10.1).

Name ______________________________

Hobby (a) ______________ (b) ______________

Skill: (a) ______________ (b) ______________

Food: ______________ Movie: ______________

Fig. 10.1 Name tags

10.1.2 Praising Is Good, and I Like It

The therapist asks each participant to look at the person next to them and choose something about them that they think appropriate to compliment upon. The therapist then asks everyone to observe and evaluate the quality of the compliment and how it was given (direction of gaze, verbal and nonverbal expressiveness, conciseness, aspect chosen for the compliment, etc.) After the first compliment, the therapist should observe whether the requirements were met and gives feedback on the *complimenting* by drawing attention to the positive aspects of the behavior. The therapist should also check if the receiver thanked the other person properly, accepting the compliments without any explanation and without denying them the compliment. If this was done, the therapist should bring attention to this by giving feedback to the one who was praised; if not, he/she should briefly talk about the importance of accepting and thanking a compliment and then resume the activity with others. In addition to giving feedback themselves, the therapist can ask someone in the group to do it, either to who was giving compliments or to whoever received them. Depending on the size of the group, the therapist can ask pairs to praise each other. He/she can also resort to pairs if someone has difficulty in selecting something from the other one to compliment them on.

10.1.3 Observing

Participants form a circle in the classroom, leaving a space in the center. The facilitator asks the participants to walk around this space without touching or bumping into each other. After a few seconds, the facilitator asks everyone to walk: on tiptoe (about 30 s) and then on their heels (30 s). He/she then asks each one to discreetly choose and observe someone in the group. The sequence is repeated, and then participants go back to walking normally. Then, the same task is done again observing a classmate while they walk. After this, the facilitator checks (a) whether the observed person identified who was observing him/her; (b) in which condition it was easier to observe; and (c) if the fact that they were being observed affected their behavior.

10.1.4 Dancing to the Tune

The facilitator plays some lively music and encourages the participants to accompany it using their body, the rhythm of the music, dancing or moving their arms and other parts of the body, or even *conducting* the movements of the group according to the music. After some time, he/she tells the participants that the music will stop, and they should all stand still or, in other words, freeze when the music stops. The facilitator touches the participants to see if they can stay still like statues. Then he/she plays some more music (slow), in which the group should react in an opposite way, i.e., very relaxed, moving around slowly. Afterwards, the facilitator alternates the two pieces of music requiring the participants to respond quickly. As an alternative, this experiential activity can be done in pairs.

10.1.5 Eye Contact

The facilitator first asks the participants to walk around the classroom to the sound of slow music, avoiding walking in a circle. Meanwhile, he/she observes how everyone is using eye contact. The facilitator stops the music by asking the participants to stand still. He/she tells the group about his/her observations concerning walking and eye contact and stresses the importance of eye contact and differences in gender, age, and social class. He/she then asks the group to walk again to the sound of a livelier song, and each participant should maintain eye contact while passing each other. The activity should now get faster. The facilitator stops the music, asks everyone to return to their seats, and checks to see if anyone found it difficult to maintain eye contact. If any participant reports any difficulties, they are instructed and asked to practice this skill.

10.1.6 Bonding with Your Group

The facilitator asks the group to stand up and get in a line, where each person is touching the next one's shoulder. He/she then asks them to synchronize a slow movement to the left and right as if they were a pendulum. When *they* are all together in this movement, the facilitator asks them to close their eyes and feel what it is like to be a group.

10.1.7 In Someone Else's Shoes

The therapist or facilitator asks everyone to walk around the classroom. Then he/she asks them to take on roles, trying to think and feel like the characters they have embodied: the role of their parents, children they have or will have, a pregnant woman, their own mother while pregnant with them, waiting for the birth, etc. Each one of these roles can be done separately, discussing and analyzing their feelings, sensations, and thoughts associated with them. If the group expresses a desire to discuss the experiential activity, the facilitator can accept briefly reflecting on each one's experience.

10.1.8 Doing Good Is Good

The facilitator asks the participants to close their eyes and be silent, relax, and imagine that they are in a nice place, doing something they know how to do very well (an activity, a game, a conversation with someone, etc.). After some time, the facilitator asks them to open their eyes and tell each other what they imagined. Then he/she asks them to relax again and imagine themselves doing something good for someone else. After a while, he/she interrupts the process and asks what the difference was between the first and second moments.

10.1.9 Watch Where You Step

The facilitator asks the group to walk barefoot around the room, trying to observe how their feet feel on the floor. Then he/she changes his requests, always waiting a few seconds for the group to try what is suggested: imagine walking on (a) rocks, (b) soft grass, (c) hot asphalt, and (d) the surface of the moon without gravity. At the end, ask them to describe the sensations and changes that they experienced in the postures.

10.2 Experiential Activities for the Key Part of the Session

10.2.1 Self-Monitoring

Objectives

Recognize that behaviors have consequences.
Identify consequences for behavior.
Make choices based on the consequences.
Illustrative video of interaction (we suggest an excerpt from the movie *As Good as It Gets* where the main character takes his girlfriend to dinner).

Material

- Supporting text.

My Behavior Affects Other People and Also Affects Me
Parents and teachers try to teach children that behaviors have consequences in the physical and social environment. Some consequences of our behavior in the physical environment are apparently easy to observe. For example, cutting down a tree where there is only one in a restricted situation. However, assessing the possible consequences of cutting down many trees in a forest can be more complicated.

In the social environment, the consequence of someone's behavior is the behavior of the other. For example, Paul greets Frank, *Good morning, Frank*, and he replies by saying, *Good morning, Paul*. Any observer may infer that (a) the two people know each other; (b) the person called Paul took the initiative in the interaction; and (c) seemingly the behaviors were similar and can be classified as greetings social skills.

As in the example, some social behaviors lead to an almost immediate identification of the consequences. That is the case for behaviors such as approaching someone, among people who know each other, the skills to ask and answer questions, greet each other, offer a seat for someone to sit down, accept the offer of some food, call attention to something that happened, and so on.

Procedure

The therapist/facilitator makes a brief explanation based on the supporting text. Then he/she asks the group to identify positive or negative consequences for some behaviors such as (a) asking for permission to enter a room; (b) playing a prank on a friend; and (c) offering to collaborate in an activity to support victims of a storm.

To conclude the activity, the therapist presents a short video and asks the participants to identify how the behavior of each of the interlocutors affected the others.

10.2.2 Self-Evaluation

Objectives

- Specific

  Describe their own behavior.
  Identify components of the interpersonal task.

Analyze the antecedents and consequences of behavior.
Recognize feelings that affect the interaction.
Talk about yourself.

- Complementary

  Identify pleasant situations and challenging or difficult situations.
  Identify rewarding and aversive behaviors.
  Share situations, difficulties, and interpersonal facilities.

Material

- Supporting questions on self-evaluation:

  1. In which situations am I satisfied with my social behavior?
  2. In which situations am I dissatisfied with my social behavior?
  3. Which behaviors of my colleagues and friends are most rewarding to me?
  4. Which of my behaviors are the most rewarding for people around me?
  5. Which of my behaviors are the most unpleasant for people around me?

- Procedure

The facilitator starts by asking the participants to relax. Then he/she gives them the worksheet and asks them to individually answer the questions on the list, without talking to anyone. Then, he/she asks each one to read out their answer to the first question, paying attention to the similarities among the participants. The same is done with each of the following questions. After this step, the facilitator asks someone in the group to explain which responses were the most similar and the most unexpected or different.

Observations

- The interpersonal homework task should be the object of attention at the beginning of the next session, where the facilitator uses the procedures of this activity.
- The facilitator should discreetly write down the names of participants who are finding it difficult to talk about themselves, trying to help them overcome this difficulty using personalized tasks and/or other experiential activities.

Variations

- An interesting variation is to do the experiential activity as a panel format, asking half or part of the group to come to the front, while the others are in charge of asking the questions, then vice versa.

- Another variation is to use the context of *put someone in the hot seat* but with two or three participants in the center and the rest around them in a circle. Someone from the circle can time how long each participant sitting in the center takes to answer the questions.

10.2.3 Self-Knowledge

Objectives

- Specific

  Observe other's behaviors.
  Observe/describe aspects of one's own behavior (self-monitoring).
  Give positive feedback to a colleague.
  Deal with evaluation received from others.
  Develop self-awareness.
  Develop self-esteem.

- Complementary

  Differentiate cognitive, affective, and behavioral aspects of yourself and others.
  Understand the relationship between these aspects.

Material

- Cards with the names of all participants
- Evaluation form (Tables 10.1 and 10.2).

Table 10.1 Self-evaluation form

I see myself as...	I think others see me as...
BEHAVIORAL DIMENSION	BEHAVIORAL DIMENSION
COGNITIVE DIMENSION	COGNITIVE DIMENSION
AFFECTIVE DIMENSION	AFFECTIVE DIMENSION

Table 10.2 Partner's evaluation form

How I see _______	How I think _______ sees him/herself
BEHAVIORAL DIMENSION	BEHAVIORAL DIMENSION
COGNITIVE DIMENSION	COGNITIVE DIMENSION
AFFECTIVE DIMENSION	AFFECTIVE DIMENSION

Procedure

In the first step, the facilitator gives the self-evaluation form to each participant and asks them to fill it in, prioritizing the positive aspects, but not showing it to the others.

Afterwards, the facilitator gives out the partner's evaluation form randomly, already with the names on it but taking care that no one receives their own.

He/she asks them to fill in the two columns but only with positive aspects. After completing the columns, he/she asks everyone to describe the classmate they evaluated based on column 1 (*How I see* ____) and then column 2 (*How I think* ____ *sees him/herself*), asking the classmate not to respond but just listen.

In the third step, the facilitator asks each participant to explain to the group (a) what he/she learned about him/herself, (b) what differences were perceived between the self-evaluation and the evaluation received from classmates, (c) what was new, and (d) what was considered the most important positive aspect about him/herself.

At the end, the facilitator discusses the issue of self-knowledge and how much it depends on our relationships with other people. He/she also discusses the importance of recognizing one's own skills and qualities and recognizing and valuing those of others.

Observations

- The facilitator should prevent negative evaluations in both the first and second stages.

Variations

- Depending on the group, the facilitator can ask for a positive aspect and one aspect to be improved, both in the self-evaluation and in the evaluation by the other.

10.2.4 Dealing with Preoccupation and Stress

Objectives

- Specific

  Understand the meaning of the term *preoccupation*.
  Recognize tensions related to preoccupation.
  Identify beliefs that can lead to avoidance of worrying situations.
  Improve self-knowledge.

- Complementary

  Identify some of the most common situations that worry you.
  Recognize that preoccupation leads to stress.
  Identify relationship problems as a source of stress.
  Learn how to relax.
  Identify coping responses to preoccupation and stress.

Material

- Supporting text

Considerations About Stress

- Preoccupation means an anticipated action (pre = before, occupation = action, i.e., occupied in advance), not at the time and place. This action primarily involves thoughts but is not restricted to them, as it also involves the body. When a person creates and recreates a situation in their thoughts (in terms of who is involved and their behaviors), this also creates bodily tension.
- Constant worry is a symptom of stress, and the major sources of stress are (a) unsatisfactory relationships, (b) financial uncertainty, and (c) work overload. For example, a student has an important test and spends a lot of time imagining how well they will do in the test (good or bad), the content of the test (easy or difficult), and the circumstances in which it will take place (behavior of teachers and classmates, material, etc.). This will make the person tired or irritated, and some stress may occur which will certainly influence his/her behavior in several ways such as difficulty concentrating, anxiety, memory slips, etc.
- Preoccupation does not result in anything concrete but rather expends a considerable and unnecessary amount of energy. Of course, most of the time, it is related to some real problems or even imaginary ones.
- Sometimes a preoccupation is not justified. In other words, some people may suffer because they are anticipating difficulties that may never materialize. Either way, if there is indeed a problem, the preoccupation will not, in itself, solve it until it is dealt with.
- An effective way to deal with preoccupation is to try to stop the flow of thoughts and do a reality check.
- Dealing with preoccupation does not mean cultivating either naive optimism (thinking that everything is ok when it is not) or catastrophic pessimism (thinking that everything is always worse than it actually is). Both cases make it difficult to tackle the problem.

Procedure

The facilitator asks the participants to move the chairs to the walls, creating a free space in the middle of the room. He/she asks them to walk around the room but not to bump into each other. After a few seconds, he/she asks the participants to imagine individually that they are very worried about something. If the participants do not express preoccupation on their face and body, the facilitator insists on new instructions and incentives: *That's right, show how worried you are*. He/she also praises them when he/she realizes that the group is making an effort to express preoccupation, for example, *Great, that's it!*

After some time, the facilitator changes the instructions as follows: *Now, let's express this same preoccupation as if it were a weight you are carrying in your hands, or on your head, or on your back. Walk around expressing all this burden.*

The facilitator waits again for some time and asks them to find a way of getting rid of the preoccupation (usually the participants pretend to throw the burden off themselves). The facilitator observes and values the alternatives found. At the end, he/she provides some clarifications about stress, based on the supporting text. The facilitator can also use examples or ask them to exemplify the aspects covered.

Observations

- Some people receive attention when telling family members and acquaintances about their preoccupations. When this becomes habitual, it can be a problem, and the person must learn to alternate topics of conversation that produce constructive attention.

Variations

- Participants can be asked to talk in small groups and identify alternative ways of dealing with preoccupations. These alternatives, derived from the experiences of each one, can be reported and discussed in terms of strategies to be tested.
- An alternative to help them to identify events that cause preoccupation is to write on the board some situations which tend to cause preoccupation: unemployment, university entrance examination, divorce, marriage, tests, serious illness, job interviews, etc.

10.2.5 The Silence Game

Objectives

- Specific

  Practice eye contact.
  Identify feelings experienced in an ambiguous situation.
  Observe/describe behaviors.
  Recognize the relation between situation, emotion, and behavior.
  Self-control of anxiety in new and ambiguous situations.

- Complementary

  Deal with an ambiguous situation.
  Analyze contingencies related to expressing emotions in new and ambiguous situations.
  Identify common strategies to deal with new and ambiguous situations.

Material

- Whiteboard
- Whiteboard pen

Procedure

Four or five members of the group are invited to make up an Experiential Group (EG), sitting on chairs placed next to each other in the middle of the room, facing the other group members of the Observation Group (OG). The therapist sits down in front of the EG, staring at them slowly, one by one, without any comments and with a neutral facial expression. After staring at the last participant, the facilitator does it again, and if any participants are calm, he/she continues staring. In this time of approximately 3 min, the OG continues to observe in silence, as the facilitator previously did. In general, the participants of the EG are very anxious and develop various strategies such as smiling, looking up or down, cracking their knuckles, swinging their legs, etc., to deal with the anxious situation.

The facilitator then asks each participant from the EG to assess the anxiety experienced on a scale from one to five. He/she asks someone from the OG to write down the scores on the board and for the others to report on their observations. Each participant should also talk about the strategies they used to alleviate the discomfort caused by the ambiguity of the situation and by the silence. If there are difficulties in this task, the facilitator exemplifies, helping the participant.

At the end of this phase, the facilitator asks the participant who reported the least anxiety (or someone of his or her choice, if everyone reports the same level of anxiety) to conduct the experiential activity, giving up his/her place. The participant, who is now in charge, must go through all the steps – up to evaluating the others' anxiety. At the end, the facilitator checks the participant's anxiety who conducted this final phase, comparing his/her score in the previous situation. At the end, the facilitator discusses the following with the whole group:

- Difficult, emotional everyday situations that can generate emotions such as fear and doubt
- Anxiety generated when facing new and ambiguous situations
- Habituation as a process of reducing anxiety insofar as, theoretically, coping reduces anxiety
- Using different strategies to deal with anxiety inducing situation and reduce discomfort, etc.
- Options for coping with these types of experiences

Observations

- We recommend using a scale of 1 to 5, rather than 0 to 5, for participants to assess their own anxiety, since zero is unlikely even when sleeping and relaxing.
- Generally, the person who replaces the facilitator in the second stage reports more anxiety than in the first, while the others report less anxiety when experiencing the process a second time. This is due to the need to cope with the unexpected situation and the responsibility to conduct the task (also a new activity).
- It is common in this activity for people making up the EG to start laughing or making comments. The facilitator should keep the serious expression as a model of the expected behavior of others and, if necessary, make a gesture to call for silence.

Variation

- At the end of the experiential activity, illustrations can be shown of ambiguous figures which, depending on the observer's position or how they look at them, different objects can be seen (e.g., the classic image of an ambiguous form, Rubin's vase). The purpose is to briefly illustrate the *natural* shortcomings of perception and the problems that follow.

10.2.6 Practicing Feedback

Objectives

- Specific

  Make better use of nonverbal communication.
  Make better use of gestures, body language, and facial expressions.
  Decode symbols in nonverbal communication.
  Analyze any observed contingencies.

- Complementary

  Understand the variability of non-vocalized behaviors.
  Relate nonverbal behaviors with culture.
  Praise/thank compliments.
  Answer questions.

Material

- Supporting text

Feedback Characteristics

Feedback is a type of social skill that consists of describing to the other the behavior that he/she presented. Analogous to mechanical and electronic devices, which maintain an established level of functioning thanks to the feedback process, human organisms continue to behave *fed* by feedback. In this sense, it is argued that positive feedback can have a reinforcing function. However, for feedback to work, some rules must be obeyed (Del Prette & Del Prette, 2001) regarding its characteristics.

- **Description**: the behavior should be described as it occurred (refer to what can be observed, what the person did, without inferring motivations or personal traits).
- **Contingency**: feedback should be given, as soon after the behavior as possible.
- **Parsimony**: feedback should be succinct, restricting it to describing what occurred just before the performance.
- **Orientation:** feedback should be directed to the person, calling him/her by name.
- **Form:** feedback can be verbal or written (avoiding adjectives), but also including visuals (filming what happened).

Feedback, especially positive feedback, is important in an SST program, as it is not only a social skill relevant to social competence, but it also works as a **technique for promoting** particular performance. Mediated by the therapist in the session, this practice contributes to creating a welcoming environment relatively free of aversive stimulation. In addition, it may lead participants to remain attentive to the performance of others, as they may be asked to give feedback about it at any time. Gradually, participants begin to use feedback among themselves, without the therapist's mediation and outside the training environment. Two important recommendations are:

- Emphasizing the use of **positive feedback** is important because it favors the discrimination of expected performances; negative feedback should be avoided.
- As positive **feedback is not confused with praise**, there is no need to thank the person giving it. However, in Brazilian culture there is some complimentary feedback associated with feedback, for example, *You spoke (very well) looking at the person directly,* which ultimately prompts thanks from the receiver.

- Presentation (e.g., PowerPoint) about feedback (Fig. 10.2).

Procedure

The therapist chooses some participants to make up the EG and the others to form the OG. The therapist asks someone from the OG to choose someone from the EG and watch them more closely. The therapist asks them to walk around the room the way they want terms of speed (fast or slow) and NVPC (head straight or sagging, swinging arms or straight, crossed arms or hands behind back).

After two or three min, the therapist stops and asks some members from the OG (one at a time) to describe what they saw, without identifying who they were watching. At that moment, the therapist corrects inferences, for example, *walking worried, in a confused way*, etc., insisting on the **description** of the (observable) behaviors.

The therapist invites members from the OG to participate in the EG, blindfolding them and asking them to pair up with someone from the EG. The member of the EG is asked to lead the blindfolded person. After a short time, the therapist asks the other members of the (remaining) OG to describe what they observed and the strategies they identified in the *guides*, asking them to give feedback to the guides. Then, the therapist asks the blindfolded person to also give feedback to their guide.

At the end, the therapist presents the instructional material (PPP about the feedback) and, based on the supporting text and other readings, presents the content and clears up any doubts. At the end, he/she assigns an interpersonal homework task involving giving feedback.

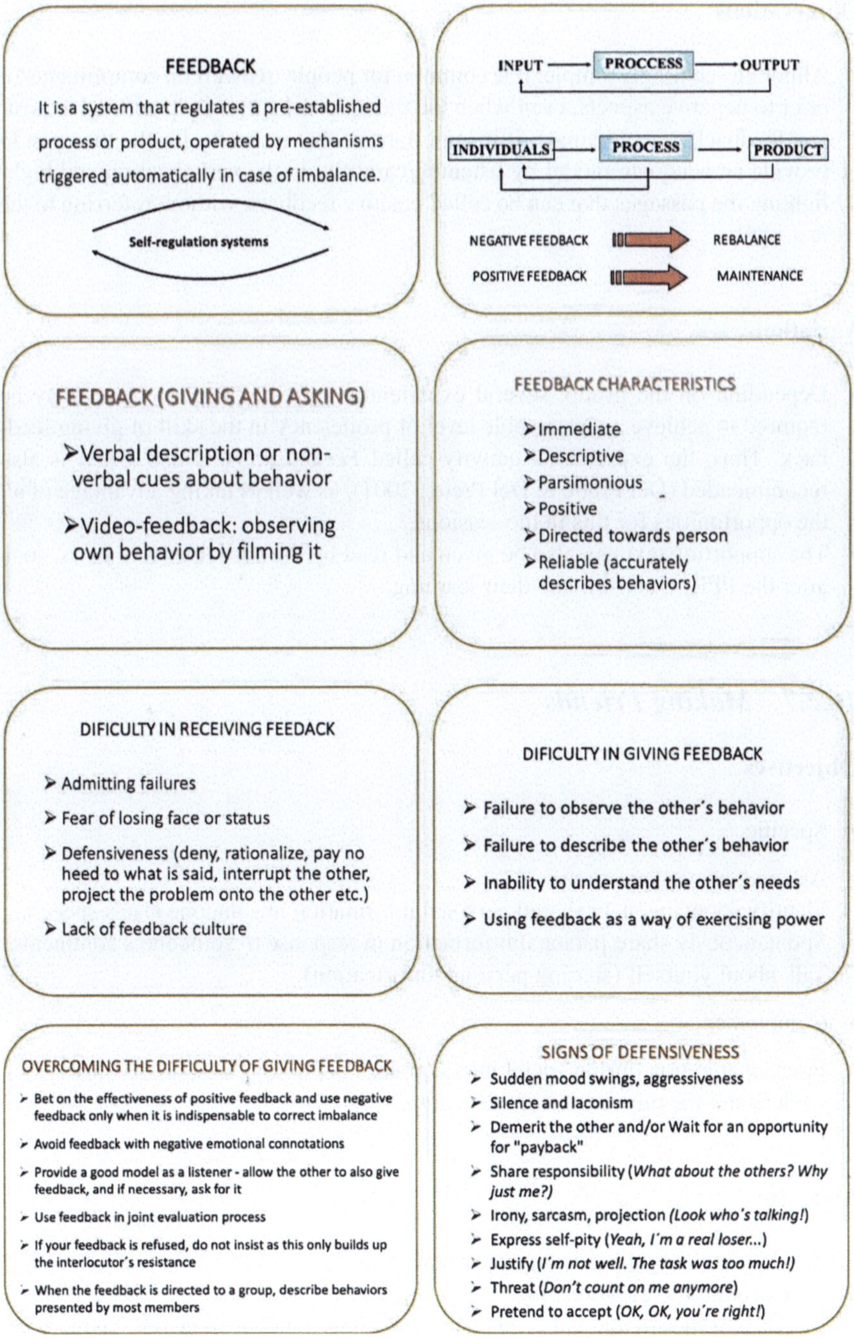

Fig. 10.2 Feedback presentation

Observations

- Although seemingly simple, it is common for people to dwell on compliments or refer to negative aspects, even when the therapist asks a participant to give positive feedback to a classmate. It is important, at that moment, for the therapist to provide an adequate model by listening carefully to the verbalization and highlighting the passages that can be called positive feedback without referring to the rest.

Variation

- Depending on the group, several experiential activities and exercises may be required to achieve an acceptable level of proficiency in the skill of giving feedback. Thus, the experiential activity called *Feedback: How and When* is also recommended (Del Prette & Del Prette, 2001), as well as taking advantage of all the opportunities for this in the sessions.
- The supporting text can also be given and read by the participants in pairs, soon after the PPP, to consolidate their learning.

10.2.7 Making Friends

Objectives

- Specific

  Ask and answer questions.
  Identify spontaneously shared personal information in someone else's speech.
  Spontaneously share personal information in response to someone's comments.
  Talk about yourself (sharing personal information).

- Complementary

  Practice attention during social interactions.
  Understand the importance of friendship.

Material

- A box containing the participants' names
- A box to put the questions in
- List of activities to maintain friendships: inviting someone to go out, giving presents, sharing problems and accomplishments, praising/encouraging, asking/offering help, giving and asking for suggestions, small talk, suggesting behav-

ioral change, giving tips about appearance (clothes, hairstyles, etc.), practicing sports together, making and accepting jokes, calling the person on the phone and showing interest in their well-being, keeping secrets, sharing pleasurable activities, taking part in events which are important for the other person (birthday, graduation ceremony, etc.), collaborating with and meeting requests, showing affection (verbal and physical)

- Question sheet (examples): **Making Friends**

1. Do you practice any kind of sport?
2. What do you usually during the weekends?
3. Which soccer team do you support?
4. Do you have any pets at home? Which ones?
5. Do you have a friend you meet up with often?
6. Do you like watching movies? What was the last movie you watched?

Procedure

The facilitator briefly checks with the group how they start friendships and which difficulties they encounter. He/she then quickly discusses strategies for starting friendships and holding a conversation with friends. The facilitator clarifies that asking/answering questions is a much-used strategy. The facilitator explains that in a conversation, open and closed questions can be used and exemplifies the difference between them. He/she highlights the importance of identifying, providing, and responding to spontaneously shared personal information, explaining what it means (see note at the end). Moreover, he/she adds other forms of approximation: comments on the weather, some current event, etc.

Then the facilitator asks each participant to choose a person from the group and pick a question from the *question box*, forming pairs for interaction. He/she gets everyone's attention and chooses one pair to act as the EG. Each person from the pair should ask a question and then continue and keep the conversation going. After a few seconds, the facilitator should stop the conversation, asking if there was any *spontaneously shared personal information* and whether or not it was used. Ask another participant from the OG to give feedback to the pair (EG) who must then return to the OG. A new pair is formed, and the facilitator proceeds similarly until everyone completes the task. At the end, he/she discusses the questions with the group that *produced* the most conversation, which were the hardest or easiest questions to answer, which difficulties they had, etc. He/she then opens up a short discussion with everyone about which questions they have already used, other questions they use, which were the most effective, and what they usually do to maintain friendships.

Observations

- In a conversation, spontaneously shared personal information includes comments that go beyond what is expected for the subject at hand. For example, someone might make the following comment: *It looks like it's going to rain*. The other confirms the prediction and adds, *Yeah, last week it rained almost every day*. Spontaneously shared personal information can be personal in nature. In this case, the person would add, *I got tired of staying inside all week*. The person who gives this information expects the other one to react to them and share something about themselves the same for the conversation to progress. If participants find it difficult to spontaneously share personal information, the experience can be repeated in another session, with explicit instructions for the exercise of this skill.
- The list of questions for this experiential activity can be used with children, couples, business colleagues, seniors, etc. In any of these cases, a previous stage can be included in which the participants think up the questions and write them on the board, selecting the best ones to put on strips of paper.
- If the group is very large, after the third pair of EG, the facilitators can (space permitting) divide the group into two, each facilitator leading one of them.

Variations

- The activity can be done twice: once without instructions or guidance regarding spontaneously shared personal information and another after such instructions. At the end, ask the group which differences there were between the first and second stage.

10.2.8 Talking Without Speaking

Objectives

- Specific

  Make better use of nonverbal communication.
  Make better use of gestures and body and facial expressions.
  Decode symbols in nonverbal communication.
  Analyze any observed contingencies.

- Complementary

  Understand the variability of non-vocalized behaviors.
  Relate nonverbal behaviors and culture.
  Praise/thank compliments.
  Answer questions.

Material

- List of popular proverbs (some examples).
  - A bird in the hand is worth two in the bush.
  - Little by little we go far.
  - Better alone than in bad company.
  - You reap what you sow!
  - Life goes on!

Procedure

The facilitator explains to the group that people communicate their feelings and desires much more through nonverbal language (body, gestures, facial expression) than through speech. He/she adds that before learning to speak, children go through an ongoing process of communicating with adults through nonverbal resources. He/she also says that the meaning of nonverbal behavior depends on culture and exemplifies this with greeting behaviors of executives in the workplace compared to teenagers at school.

Afterwards, the facilitator chooses three participants (EG) and, starting with those who have less difficulty in expressing themselves, asks them to communicate (without saying anything) something to the others (OG). They are asked to observe and decipher the meaning of the nonverbal message by raising their hand as soon as they discover what it is and tell everyone when the facilitator says.

Afterwards, he/she asks the EG members (without the others listening) to communicate (without saying anything) popular proverbs, suggesting some or asking them to suggest some themselves. If the OG cannot decode the communication, the facilitator asks the participant to do it again, making it clearer. After some attempts, two OG members are asked to give positive feedback to the behavior of each EG member. The task can be repeated with other participants, including the OG, depending on how motivated and interested they become in the exercise.

At the end, the facilitator asks the participants to give examples of everyday cultural messages that people use without uttering a word, for example, raising your hand when you want to speak, expressing *Yes*, shaking your head to say *No*, thumbs up, thumbs down, and calling someone with your hands. Others, which are more subtle, include smiling, posture, raising your eyebrows, frowning, etc. He/she also highlights the interpersonal difficulties that arise when we are unable to express ourselves nonverbally or when we do not properly decode someone's nonverbal communication.

Observations

- The facilitator can change the items on the list of proverbs by substituting or including some others.

Variations

- An alternative is to organize the communication of proverbs, in pairs, with one person of the pair initiating the phrase and the other completing it. Each pair studies and rehearses separately how they will perform their assigned proverb.
- The facilitator may present illustrations of types of gestures that have similar or even opposing meanings in different cultures.

10.2.9 What My Friend Told Me

Objectives

- Specific

  Listen to the other person, pay attention.
  Talk about yourself, open up to others.
  Get to know classmates.
  Make friends.

- Complementary

  Understand the other person.
  Recount events.

Material

- Worksheet of tips (Table 10.3).

Table 10.3 Tips for the speaker and the listener

SPEAKER'S TIPS	LISTENER'S TIPS
Look at the listener when speaking	Pay attention to what the interlocutor is saying
Do not speak too loudly or too quietly	Do not interrupt whoever is speaking, except when necessary.
Say only what happened and what you felt	Ask the interlocutor (by signalling) to speak lower or louder, if necessary.
Try to use the time available well	Avoid signs of impatience.
Do not talk about people behind their back	Avoid talking about people who are not there, so as not to shift the focus.

Procedure

The facilitator briefly discusses the importance of social life, how it allows people to share ideas, learn from each other, talk about their feelings, problems, things that happened (good or bad), things they did, etc. He/she then explains the importance of some tips that can be followed when talking and listening to someone else and posts the worksheet somewhere everyone can see it or gives one to each group.

He/she then asks the participants to come together in groups of three and for each person to talk about an event that made him/her happy or sad to the other two people. The facilitator gives them 10 min for this (depending on the group). During this time, the facilitator monitors the groups, discretely encouraging participants.

After this part has finished, the facilitator asks each group to choose only one of the three reports and then choose one of the listeners to present it to the others. He/she adds that now the narrative should be told so that everyone can hear it, preparing the group for the second stage of the experiential activity.

After the narratives, the facilitator asks the group the following questions:

- *What did you learn about your colleagues?*
- *What did each one of you feel like when you told your colleagues something personal?*
- *Who had difficulties? What kind of difficulties?*

Finally, the facilitator goes back to the initial theme, presenting feedback and emphasizing the importance of being able to communicate personal things to classmates and also the importance of listening and paying attention to others in the process of making friends.

Observations

- The facilitator can recommend the participants to continue having the same type of conversation they had in the experiential activity in other situations, even outside the session.

Variations

- In order to ensure greater integration between participants, the facilitator can either choose the groups or choose the first participant from each group, leaving them the task of choosing the remaining two.

10.2.10 Rights and Obligations

Objectives

- Recognize rights and obligations.
- Act assertively.
- Recognize organizations that defend human rights in the country.
- Identify strata of society that are treated negatively and are more disadvantaged when compared to others with greater purchasing power.
- Admit that everyone is equal before the law.

Material

- Texts with situations for exercising assertiveness

Text 1
Garret answered the doorbell to the team delivering the mattress he and his wife had finally bought. He couldn't help showing his enthusiasm and shouted out, *Maryanne, Maryanne, it's here! It's finally here!* Maryanne appeared smiling, wiping her hands on her apron and said, *Calm down, my dear! Calm down!* The delivery people were already inside the house, asking where they should put it. A few minutes later everything was settled, but when Garret decided to sit on the mattress, he almost shouted, *Uh oh! Something's wrong.* Maryanne also noticed the problem and said, *The spring seems to be broken in these two places!* The delivery men said they could not do anything. They had done their job, and the solution would be for them to cover those parts of the mattress with cloths. They got Garret's signature, said goodbye, and left. **The group should answer the following questions: (a) What could the couple have done? (b) How could the problem be solved?**

Text 2
Lily was young and a hard worker. She was asked after whenever there was a task that required reading or speaking in English, Spanish, and German. However, her salary was much lower than that of some colleagues with the same job she held. She realized that she worked harder and earned less. She thought of talking to her director, but he was always busy, and her colleagues said he did not like complaints from employees. **The group should answer the following questions: (a) How could Lily solve this problem? (b) How could she find out about the director's availability and make an appointment? (c) And if she managed, how should she explain her problem to the director?**

Text 3

Martha had been seeing David for about 3 months. She liked him but wanted to understand their situation better. When she spoke about commitment, he changed the subject and started becoming aggressive. Martha thought that in the future David would not be so bossy. The last time she talked about commitment, he was furious and even pushed her. Martha said that she did not like this aggressive behavior at all and David apologized, but also replied, *Not all this talk about marriage again!* **The group should answer the following questions: (a) Will David change his mind? (b) What could Martha do?**

Procedure

This experiential activity is divided into two stages. In the **first stage**, the therapist divides the participants into three groups. Each group is given one of three sets of texts. Each group is given the task of (a) choosing a coordinator, (b) reading the text assigned to them, (c) discussing the text, and (d) answering the questions. At the end of this phase, each group reads their text to the others and tells them the conclusions they have reached. This discussion enables the therapist to get to know what the participants' beliefs and values are like. The therapist should mediate the discussion of divergent opinions, avoiding radicalizations.

Aggressive-Assertive-Passive Reactions

- The therapist explains that, roughly speaking, when people are faced with questions, such as those they have analyzed that involve **values**, they try to express their opinion. In many social situations, people need to say what they think and feel.
- The norms taught by family members, the models that each one finds in their experiences, and the consequences that occur when people behave favoring the development of certain styles of behavior. Roughly the styles were classified into three groups: (a) passive, (b) aggressive, and (c) assertive. Usually in the passive style people prefer not to speak up and even when asked to say what they think avoid the subject and often find a way to *sit on the fence* or adopt the position held by the majority. In an aggressive style, people say what they think, defending their ideas and values, but they do it in a forceful way, without caring about the feelings of others. They often exaggerate the way they talk, shouting and making threatening gestures. In an assertive style, people also express and defend their rights, without, however, disrespecting the other's opinion. Moreover, assertiveness will be even more effective if preceded by some expression of empathy toward the needs of the other.

- Very rarely does one develop a purely passive, aggressive, or assertive style. More commonly, these styles alternate, varying according to the situation, but there may be a greater predominance of one style over the others. Think of a dotted line that the more you follow to the left, you can see more aggressiveness and on the opposite side, moving to the right, passiveness is more common. The central part of this line would be represented by assertiveness, which also oscillates toward one direction or another.

In the **second step**, the therapist begins by giving a brief explanation, considering these points about aggressive-assertive-passive:

The therapist holds a discussion of the three cases presented. In the **first case**, the therapist asks what action would be taken by the couple who bought a mattress. If necessary, he/she helps the group to conclude that it is important to look for information about the company's return policy, indicating that they believe they have some rights as consumers. He/she explains that if they already knew about their rights, they probably would not have accepted the product. Now they will have to go to the store and ask for the mattress to be replaced. Which style could achieve the best result? In the passive style, they could end up withdrawing the complaint or they could place the *complaint* in a very submissive way and the solution to the problem would be delayed, taking a long time to solve the problem.

In the **second case**, Lily recalls that she performs some tasks that others are not able to do, at least not to the full extent, which seems to make the arguments to be presented easier. The facilitator can draw attention to the question of values.

Concerning the **third case**, the therapist may argue that Martha will probably have to make a decision to break up with David. He/she explains that assertiveness often only protects the person and can avoid harmful consequences to the person.

10.2.11 Expressing Affection

The facilitator asks the participants to form a circle and choose the person who got most involved in the session, asking them to go to the middle. He/she then asks the others to express positive feelings toward him/her, first in a nonverbal way and then verbally, for example, affection, votes of confidence, courage, etc. This experiential activity is especially important to wind down experiential activities where one of the people has been subjected to more anxiety provoking demands.

10.2.12 Solving Interpersonal Problems

Objectives

- Specific

  Coordinate the group.
  Analyze the situation and define the problem.
  List and analyze alternatives to solve the problem.
  Choose the best alternative to solve the problem.

- Complementary

  Ask and answer questions.
  Give feedback.
  Evaluate behaviors.

Material

- Worksheet with a list of group coordinator's basic tasks (See Portfolio of Social Skills, Chap. 3)
- Supporting text

Dealing with Interpersonal Problems

The first requirement for solving an interpersonal problem is to answer the questions: **What is a problem? What is an interpersonal problem? What is the solution to an interpersonal problem?**

A **problem** can be defined as a mismatch between the demand for an adaptive response to a situation and the repertoire of effective responses of the person or people who need to deal with it, due to one or more obstacles. An **interpersonal** problem is a special kind of real-life problem in which the obstacle is a conflict between the behavioral demands or expectations of two or more people in a relationship.

Therefore, there is an interpersonal problem when there are conflicts in the behavioral demands and expectations between two or more people in a relationship. It can be said that some of the behaviors of one of the parties displease the other and that the expected behaviors (expectations) occur at a low frequency or do not occur.

The **solution to an interpersonal problem** is the result of a cognitive-behavioral process among those involved in the conflict which includes (a) characterizing the problem, specifying the demands and expectations; (b) identifying alternatives that have the potential to solve the problem effectively; and (c) choosing and (then) implementing the chosen alternative, which may mean changing behaviors. The result of this process must be satisfactory for all those involved. According to this perspective, and coherent with the concept of social competence already defined, the solution to interpersonal problems must therefore be governed by the *win-win* principle rather than the *win-lose* principle.

It is important to clarify that, for the most part, an interpersonal problem happens in the context of one particular situation, which makes it easier to solve. However, sometimes it can involve several situations in which the people involved come in contact with each other, which can result in emotional separation and a difficulty to do things together.

An interpersonal problem should not be confused with **a conflict**, but it can begin there. A conflict concerns people with different opinions and positions and, when the disagreement is properly discussed, can lead to interesting discoveries and even to approximation between the opponents.

Interpersonal problems happen very often, regardless of the age of those involved, and most of them are resolved without major difficulties. However, some are persistent and take longer to solve. There are cases of interpersonal problems that span generations.

Some problems develop slowly, over time, and others may suddenly erupt. In the first case, a latent divergence is often perceived but not yet manifested between the parties. When the conflict arises, it can be perceived by the people involved, other group members, and even people outside the group. Interpersonal situations may be potentially problematic when those involved have conflicting interests, are prejudiced, intolerant, and/or have difficulties in negotiating.

In short, a problem is not when the conflict occurs but in the way it is managed and dealt with. Some steps can be brought up as part of the solution to a problem in response to some questions: (a) What is the problem or how is it characterized? (b) Which people are involved in the problem? (c) Do those involved want to solve the problem? If the problem is seen as a way of overcoming something, it can be an opportunity for rebalancing power, an important learning opportunity for those directly involved and those who are only observing the problem-solving in action.

- Items for directing the OG's observation of the EG

1. Write down dispersive or negative, pessimistic, and uncooperative behaviors (changing the subject, showing irritation, interrupting someone).
2. Identify who redirects the conversation back toward a focus on the problem (returning to topic, asking relevant questions, giving suggestions).
3. Who is demonstrating through their postures or gestures that they are listening attentively (looking at the speaker, nodding, signaling understanding, asking for explanations)?

4. Who is helping solve the problem (making suggestions, giving/asking for examples, drawing attention to the subject at hand)?
5. Three sheets of paper, each one with a problem described at the top and the rest left blank for the group to use.

- Interpersonal problems for analyses

Problem 1
Peter Saunders is an industry manager and supervises various teams. In addition to routine activities (such as distributing tasks, participating in projects, organizing data sheets, attending meetings with directors, responding to and sending memos, supervising and checking documents, etc.), he also supervises teams. His direct contact with each employee is restricted to greetings and brief comments when they meet occasionally. In his last meeting with the director, he was told there was a problem, which was the following: *Peter, you have an employee in your team, Mr. F who is said to be competent and dedicated. F's colleagues avoid him and complain that he has bad BO (body odor). The leader of the group brought the problem to our attention, but no one was willing to face this situation. It is up to you to resolve this.* THE GROUP MUST (1) analyze the problem and arrive at a solution and (2) list some social skills required to solve this problem.

Problem 2
Paul Ryan was assigned to manage a team that had its ups and downs in terms of productivity. The analysis of the performance chart of each team member was very similar. Upward and downward trends were almost simultaneous for everyone, even when the work was independent. The team could barely meet its goals, the organizational climate was sometimes poor, and there was a lot of criticism and jokes in poor taste among the staff. ACCORDING TO THE GROUP: What should Paul do?

Problem 3
Anthony Pearson was very dedicated to his work. Over the past few months, he contributed significantly to the team's achievement of its goals. He often had interesting suggestions, but he could not always make himself heard. When he proposed an idea, it took a long time to get any attention from even one person, and when he was able to say something, the subject that was being discussed had already changed, and the others had turned their attention to another topic. When the moment was right, he would lose himself in talking about his ideas, repeating ideas, justifying himself, and even stammering. Some of his colleagues were often amused and tried to hide their laughter. For this very reason, Anthony preferred to be quiet or to agree with his colleagues' ideas when it was the case. GROUP TASK: How can we help Anthony Pearson?

Procedure

For this experiential activity, the facilitator organizes two EG groups and two OG groups. In the first phase of the experience, he/she requests that each EG chooses its coordinator and spokesperson. Then, he/she gives the coordinators the sheet with the problem, instructing the group to (a) read it in silence; (b) define the problem by writing it down; (c) discuss alternatives to solve the problem; (d) note down possible solutions; and (e) choose the best solution for the activity.

In each OG group, the facilitator gives one of the people the LIST OF THE COORDINATOR'S BASIC TASKS asking them to look for these aspects; he/she hands out specific questions that help direct the other member's observation.

The facilitator sets a time of 20 min for the EG to reach a solution to the problem. During this time, he/she monitors them, checking each one's participation and, if necessary, provides clues, without, however, giving any answers. When the time is up, the facilitator asks each coordinator to recount the aspects noted down by the group and present them to the others. During the presentation, he/she asks the others to give positive feedback to the account given.

The facilitator presents aspects of the supporting text about problem-solving and inverts the members of the EG and OG condition. In this situation, he/she whispers to a member of each EG to present *negative* and *dispersive* behaviors, respectively.

Once the time is up, he/she proceeds to discuss the task once again, this time highlighting the coordinator's behaviors in order to control dispersion and negativity. At the end, he/she discusses the importance of applying the problem-solving process, both in the individual and group context. Moreover, he/she values the coordinators' and observers' positive aspects.

Observations

- Depending on the group's resources and the objectives, the facilitator may choose to present the supporting text at the beginning of this experiential activity and not in the middle as described.

Variations

- The facilitator can use other problem cases, chosen for their potential to instigate the problem-solving process.

10.2.13 *Never the Same*

Objectives

- Specific

  Develop behavioral flexibility in everyday interpersonal relationships.
  Develop creativity though alternative behaviors for the same situation.
  Analyze everyday social interactions.
  Coordinate the group.

- Complementary

  Give feedback.
  Identify routine everyday situations.

Material

- Paper and pencil
- Poster with LIST OF COORDINATOR'S BASIC TASKS (See Portfolio of Social Skills, Chap. 3)

Procedure

The facilitator explains to the group that one of the objectives of this and some experiential activities, including this one, within the program is to improve the repertoire of social skills and increase the number of alternatives available for various social situations experienced in daily life. He/she adds that many social situations remain fairly similar and require reactions with few possibilities of variation, for example, buying a newspaper from the newspaper stand, answering a question about the time, etc. He/she asks the group for examples of other interpersonal tasks in which our behavior presents little variability without hindering the achievement of any objectives.

He/she also states that, on the other hand, in more complex situations, we tend to repeat the same behaviors when greater variability would be desirable. He/she asks for examples of social situations that may require alternative behaviors, both to prevent the relationship from deteriorating and to achieve the goals of the interpersonal tasks involved. He/she provides examples of situations and demands (speaking in a work meeting, helping a classmate, making friends) in which the absence of variability can hinder favorable outcomes for the two interlocutors or even lead to undesirable outcomes.

After this presentation, the facilitator asks the group to divide themselves into pairs or small groups of three participants. For half of the groups, he/she asks them to come up with an example where (a) the situation is almost the same most of the time and (b) the participants' behaviors almost invariably repeat themselves. In addition, each group should list the required social skills for this situation. For the other groups, he/she asks them to come up with an example of a situation which is (a) unusual in people's lives and (b) at least two alternatives to deal with such situations.

During the task, the facilitator supervises the groups, helping them discreetly. Afterwards, he/she then instructs each group to talk about their work, choosing a spokesperson for this task. At each presentation, the others should provide positive feedback to the group. The facilitator also asks someone to report an experience in which he/she did not achieve this variability and another in which he/she achieved good variability and outcomes.

Observation

- This experiential activity can also be carried out with groups of couples, leading to important discoveries and insights. The facilitator may suggest variability as an interpersonal homework task for all or only a few participants, depending on the progress of the group.

Variations

- To illustrate the inconvenience of routine in relationships, the facilitator can divide the participants into small groups and ask them to analyze some lyrics (e.g., *Monotony*, by Sofi Tyler https://www.youtube.com/watch?v=6naHkuFZVC4 – accessed on 24/11/18) or movies (e.g., *As Good as It Gets* with Jack Nicholson). After the analysis, each group recounts their work, receiving feedback from the others and from the facilitator.
- Another interesting variation, depending on the repertoire of the participants, is to ask each group to present their work by drawing it for the others, and afterwards they discuss (a) problems associated with behavioral rigidity and (b) importance of adapting possible alternatives to the context of the interaction.

10.2.14 Social Interaction Values

Objectives

- Specific

  Identify behaviors that reflect values.
  Reflect on values relevant to the coexistence between people.
  Observe and report behaviors.
  Give opinions about values.

- Complementary

  Make comparisons and analyses.
  Develop self-monitoring.

Material

- Worksheets describing interpersonal situations that may involve values
  1. P found a wallet with money in it. He checked the identity card. He found the owner's address and went there immediately to return it.
  2. J heard two neighbors commenting that Mariana, who lived in house number 37 on the same street, had taken Tony's (Jill's son) stroller to her house. He knew this was not true. What did Jill do?
  3. Gerald was angry with Lucy, his girlfriend, because he saw her affectionately saying goodbye to a good-looking guy. He thought about facing up to her but ended up sending a message to Lucy cancelling their date.
- Values of coexistence table (Fig. 10.3)

Kindness	Reciprocity	Creativity	Equality	Gratitude
Respect	Courage	Honesty	Cooperation	Commitment
Ethics	Health	Power	Responsibility	Discipline
Humility	Affection	Compassion	Generosity	Knowledge
Tolerance	Persistence	Freedom	Justice	Goodness
Audacity	Autonomy	Beauty	Solidarity	Forgiveness

Fig. 10.3 Frame of values

Procedure

For the first step, the facilitator asks the participants to organize themselves into groups and asks each group to choose a coordinator and a spokesperson. He/she gives each group the values of coexistence table and asks them to check if they would include any more. He/she asks them to choose the most meaningful for them, ranking them in order from the most important to the least. Each group should choose the three values they ranked the most important and discuss situations in which these values emerge in interactions between people. Then, the facilitator gives each group the list of interpersonal situations and asks them to decide as a group which values are associated with each one.

For the second step, the facilitator asks each group to explain what they have produced and then writes down, on the board, the values ranked the highest by the groups and the situations to which they were associated. He/she then asks them to choose one of the scenarios to act out the two extremes: an interaction oriented by that value and one oriented by opposing values or disregarding that value.

At the end, the facilitator conducts a relaxation activity with the participants asking them to close their eyes and imagine their family, friends, and acquaintances living in harmony and respecting the values they considered most important. He/she chooses some people to say what they imagined.

Observations

- Emphasis should be on positive values of coexistence, but if a participant insists on any questionable value (e.g., ambition, power), the facilitator may ask the group to discuss short- and long-term advantages and disadvantages of relationship patterns oriented toward these values.

Variations

- The facilitator can also create interpersonal situations where values of coexistence create conflict over immediate outcomes and medium- and long-term outcomes (e.g., honesty can lead a person to report a shortcoming, and dishonesty can mean they prefer the immediate result of lying).

10.2.15 Let's Get to Know Peter

Objectives

- Specific

  Differentiate fact from interpretation, impression, or judgment.
  Recognize factors that influence opinions and judgments.
  Identify influences of the situation and culture on social perception.
  Identify cultural judgments and prejudices.
  Recognize preconceptions in everyday interactions.
  Avoid hasty judgments based on others' impressions.

- Complementary

  Understand the diversity of opinions and judgments.
  Self-observe and notice ones' own prejudices and judgments.
  Expose judgments that contradict those of the group.

Material

- Paper and pencil
- Supporting text for the facilitator: PERCEPTION, JUDGMENT, AND PREJUDICE (see Joana's story)
- Cards with the accounts of people related to Peter (one version for each group) and Peter 's own version (for the facilitator)

Text 1 – Peter, My Son
I had trouble waking Peter up this morning. Finally, he got up, washed his face, got ready, and ran to the table. It seemed to me that he was hungry as he ate two slices of bread with butter and drank all the tea I'd made for him. He's fussy; he doesn't like coffee. Do you know anyone who doesn't like freshly brewed coffee? After that, he grabbed his backpack, checked to see if he had his workbook, said goodbye, and ran to the bus stop. He didn't kiss me like he used to. Children grow up and are ashamed of their parents. I noticed, when he left, that his shoes were worn out; his left shoe already had a hole in the sole. That's what you get for kicking everything in sight. After this mother's report, what does the group think of Peter?

Text 2 – Peter, My Best Friend
When Peter arrived, I was already at the bus stop. I showed him my new superhero stickers. Peter turned his head, looked at them, and made no comment. This guy does not like collecting superhero stickers; he only thinks about soccer. I put my stickers away, and Peter asked if I had my workbook. I said yes, but I hadn't finished the exercises the teacher had given for homework. I asked if I could copy his from his workbook, but he didn't answer me. He just kept avoiding my question. Finally, he said that if I didn't do it myself, I wouldn't learn. I think Peter listens too much to Mark who's a stuck-up guy. I already told him he's going to get stuck up too. Looks like he didn't take my warning seriously. That's what we get for trying to help. After this friend's account, what does the group think of Peter?

Text 3 – Peter, the Passenger on the Bus I Drive
It was the last but one stop when those boys got on the bus. Luke got on the bus quickly. The other one took a long time just to wind me up. When he got on, he said *Good morning.* I didn't answer. I know his game, first he's late, and then pretends he's polite. He was whistling, as if he was making fun of me. I kept an eye on him in the mirror. Shirt not tucked in, cap turned to the side, I don't know what will become of this kid. I noticed that his backpack was larger than usual. Though he tried to hide it, putting it under the seat, it looked like he was carrying a ball. When we got to the bus stop near the school, the kids came down, and I saw that it really was a ball inside his backpack. A thief is a thief, whether he steals a dime or a diamond. After the bus driver's report, what does the group think of Peter?

Text 4 – Peter, My *Crush*
My name's Marina. I'm in the fifth grade. My classmates are very annoying. I met a boy from fourth grade who's pretty cool. He is a friend of Luke's and Emmett's, but the three are never together. Peter looks so cool when he turns his cap to one side. He lives far away from my house. Ivy told me that he lives in the slums and that he must be a pothead. I don't know if this is true! We arrived at the same time today. I stared at him. He glanced over and then put his head down. He doesn't get it! Then he ran to meet Emmett. I noticed Emmett had something in his hand that could have been a cigarette. I also saw Luke frowning, maybe because they didn't ask him to smoke with them. I think they' re going to get into some kind of trouble. I already wrote a note to Peter, but I didn't have the guts to send it. After Marina's report, what does the group think of Peter?

Text 5 – Peter, My Classmate
I'm Peter's classmate, and my name's Emmett. He doesn't like talking much. The other day I said to him, *Let's smoke in the bathroom.* He didn't even answer. Some people like him. Today he came with a ball in his backpack. I know he's got Alfred's ball because Alfred said yesterday that his ball went missing. Then I went to talk to Peter, asking for the ball to play. He said he didn't have a ball. Cheeky! Then I shouted, *Thief, thief!* He didn't react, grabbed his backpack, and ran off. As it was time for recess, he met up with Luke and then kept looking over at Marina, showing off. My dad always says that silence means consent. I went to the teacher and told her everything. She just listened, then said she was going to check out some things with him. After this classmate's report, what does the group think of Peter?

Text 6 – Peter, My Student

I can't work Peter out. Sometimes he seems to be an intelligent boy, he answers the questions I ask him, but at other times he is oblivious, as if he were in another world. The other day he said that this war between the United States and Iran was good for people who make bombs, who got even richer. I thought it was a smart answer. In another class, he spent a lot of his time drawing. I was very angry and confiscated his drawing. On one side were the names of his classmates organized into two teams for a soccer game. On the other side was a drawing that I just didn't understand: one figure on top of the other. It looks like someone crazy did it. I heard from Emmett that he stole a classmate's ball and brought it to school. This is very serious. I hope everything will become clear. After the teacher's report, what does the group think of Peter?

Text 7 – Peter, Himself

It was difficult for me to get up this morning. On Sunday I helped Alfred and his father sell sugarcane juice in front of the soccer field. It was exhausting. My mother was nice; she made some mint tea that hit the spot. I met my friend, Luke, at the bus stop who lives near here. He showed me a new sticker of his. Then, Luke asked to copy my homework. He's my friend, but I don't think that was alright because if he copies, he'll never learn. I told him that. Suddenly, the bus arrived, stopping a little way from the bus stop. I tried to run. My leg hurt, and I was the last one to get on. I said hello to Joe, the driver. He didn't answer. I think there was a lot of noise and he couldn't hear, otherwise he would have answered. It was incredible that our bus arrived alongside Marina's. She's a nice girl, I really like her, but I don't know if she's interested in me. Then Mark arrived, and I couldn't see Marina anymore. The teacher kept looking at me the whole class. I don't know why. During recess it all went pear shaped. Emmett came and asked me for a ball. I said I didn't have a ball, that the one in the backpack was not mine. He called me a thief. I wanted to punch him, but what saved me was that it was time for me to return the ball to Alfred that I had borrowed. He had two balls; one had gone missing. Even so, he lent me the other one, so I could play. Alfred is nice. I ran to take the ball to Alfred and ran into Marina. I don't know what happened; all the anger I felt disappeared. I looked at her and wanted to *flirt*. I got the ball, and I started doing keepie-uppies. I'm really good at this. When the bell rang, I went back to the classroom. The teacher came over and told me she wanted to talk to me. I wonder what she wants?

Procedure

In preparation for the experiential activity, the facilitator should study the supporting text and prepare to use its content with the participants.

To begin the experiential activity, the facilitator divides the participants into six groups of four or five participants and recommends that each group elect a coordinator and a spokesperson. After that, he/she gives each group one of the first six texts, handing out a copy to each participant. The groups are asked to read in silence and then discuss and answer the questions at the end of the text on a sheet of paper, according to the group's shared understanding of what they read. The groups will be identified by the numbers of the texts (one, two, three, and so on), and each answer sheet should contain all the group participants' names, as well as indicate who was chosen as coordinator and spokesperson.

The facilitator should give approximately 15 min (depending on the group) to complete this part. During this phase, the facilitator monitors the groups, helping without influencing their responses, and especially supporting the coordinator and spokesperson.

When the time is up, the facilitator explains that each group will, in a moment, read their text and tell everyone their impression of Peter and that it is important that everyone else listens, as the text and the interpretation of the previous group may bring additional elements to the analysis that they themselves made based on their own text.

The facilitator writes the groups' numbers on the board. Then, they may begin the next stage, following a sequence of steps:

1. Ask Group 1 to read their text and share their interpretation of it (monitoring the others so that they only listen without engaging in parallel conversations or reacting too openly).
2. Say to the others: *Does any group want to change their interpretation based on Group One's analysis?* Wait a little while and then write on the board, next to the group number, only YES for those who changed their interpretation.
3. Ask Group 2 to read their text and to share their interpretation of it (monitoring the others so that they only listen without engaging in parallel conversations or reacting too openly).
4. Ask the others again if they would change and write YES next to the group number that says they would.

The facilitator proceeds in the same way with all the groups. In the case of those who indicated change, when they present their own analysis, he/she asks them to also comment on their initial analysis and the changes made to it. When everyone has already explained their analysis, he/she asks if any group want to change something based on previous reports.

When all of the groups have presented, the facilitator reads the last text (*Peter himself*), asking for everyone's attention. After reading it, he/she asks questions focusing on aspects of the content of each text and others about the differences in judgments that appeared between the report of the boy himself and the different positions of the groups:

- *Did Marina mind that Peter lived in the slums?*
- *Why did Emmett call Peter a thief?*
- *Why aren't our judgments always correct?*
- *Does anyone have an example of having made a wrong judgment about someone?*
- *Why is a person who lives in a slum judged more negatively than a resident of another neighborhood?*
- *Do residents who live in good neighborhoods make mistakes? What are the facts and what are the judgments found in the texts?*
- *Did the group base Peter's story on facts or judgments?*
- *Which judgments about Peter were positive and which were negative?*

At this point, the facilitator gives the following instruction: *The texts that you received contained some* ***descriptive*** *passages (facts) and interpretative passages (judgments). Each group should identify in their text which parts are facts and which are judgments.* If necessary, the facilitator explains in more detail what is an observable fact and what is the interpretation of a fact. He/she gives them a few minutes for the task and asks each group to report the facts and then interpretations, asking others to confirm or disagree, if necessary.

He/she then asks each group to explain which excerpts or words from the text are facts (an account of events narrated by people regarding Peter) and which are impressions or interpretations of facts. Finally, the facilitator discusses the experiential activity with the groups, based on the following questions:

- *What are Peter's positive and negative aspects?*
- *Were the analyses based on facts or judgments for your task of outlining Peter's profile?*
- *What happens on a day-to-day basis when we mistake judgments for facts? What are the consequences of this?*
- *How is it possible to change the harmful effects of this practice?*
- *At the end of the experience, the facilitator gives a short presentation based on the facilitator's supporting text.*

Observations

- If the group is very large, the facilitator should evaluate the possibility of forming groups with six participants or else create one or two extra groups, repeating texts 5 and 6 with them. Comparing the analyses of the same texts can enrich the experiential activity.
- In the texts a lot of slang was used, typical of some current contexts. They can be changed according to the characteristics of the groups.
- Often, the groups that analyze texts 3, 4, and 6 are those that make more serious judgments regarding Peter. The facilitator should not express an attitude of disapproval but rather allow the experiences to serve as a reflection for the participants.

Variations

- Text 7, *Peter himself*, can also be given to a group, adopting the same procedure in relation to the others.

10.2.16 Joana's Story

Objectives

- Specific

  Develop values of coexistence.
  Differentiate fact from interpretation, impression, or judgment based on facts.
  Recognize factors that influence opinions and judgments.
  Identify cultural judgments and prejudices.
  Recognize preconceptions in everyday interactions.
  Avoid hasty judgments, based on reports of others' impressions.

- Complementary

  Understand/accept the diversity of opinions and judgments.
  Self-analyze trying to identify possible prejudices and judgments.
  Expose judgments that contradict those of the group.

- Develop self-monitoring

Material

- Paper and pencil
- Supporting text for facilitator

Perception, Judgment, and Prejudice
From childhood, we have learned to identify people based on biological differences (man, woman, tall, thin) or on the roles they play in society (doctor, teacher, mother, father, student). Our learning becomes more complex when we make specific distinctions within a general class, for example, in the case of fathers, there is our father, John's father, Mary's father, Alfred's father, all of which we need to distinguish between.

When we meet someone for the first time, we make a mental picture of them based on some of their characteristics that attract the most attention: this is what we call **social perception**. Based on this perception, we make a judgment that can be positive or negative. This judgment is influenced by beliefs (what we think) and feelings. **Social judgment** is also learned and almost always follows perception. Our judgments of others are passed on to others, who may or may not accept them or who can demystify them when they are not justified or incorrect.

Judgments are also influenced by the identification we have with our group. First, we identify with our parents, then with the family group (siblings, uncles and aunts, grandparents), with groups of friends, religious groups, leisure, work, ethnic group, etc. (at this moment, the therapist should give several examples of these groups). The notion of being part of a group includes the perception that others (known or not) are not part of it.

In this process we tend to value our own group and devalue the group of others: *my* family, *my* team, *my* school, are the best. This is the basis for learning negative prejudice. Differences between people are common, but they should not be treated in a judgmental and evaluative sense. The big problem is when we relate to people based on an initial judgment and, thus, fail to see any facts that could change that judgment.

Perception and judgment are natural processes in the life of the human being. They can become a problem when they are distorted by negative prejudices that prevent us from seeing reality as it really is. In this case, judgments are more difficult to change.

- Cards with accounts of people related to Joana (one version for each group) and Joana's own version (for the facilitator)

Text 1. Joana, My Daughter
Joana got up as usual on this particular day. She got ready quickly, had a cup of tea with a slice of bread, refusing the butter I make at home. She's always thinking about her diet. She grabbed her things and also refused to listen to me when I told her to take a coat. I've noticed that she's been pensive lately. She doesn't obey me anymore. I think she does some things just to go against me. She's a good girl deep down inside, still a child, although she's in her twenties and despite modern times. **Based on Joana's mother's report, the group should outline Joana's profile based on her traits and characteristics.**

Text 2. Joana, My Friend
The doorbell rang three times. I knew it was Joana, always in a hurry. I ran to the door, kissed her on the cheek, and took the elevator down with her to the first floor. She didn't utter a single word nor did she respond to Arthur's compliment, a young man from the neighborhood who likes her. Joana is more reserved. I noticed, however, that she was wearing a very low-cut blouse. I often wonder if Joana is not having an affair with someone. Just hope she doesn't mess with my hot boyfriend. She's got this innocent face that all men like. When we left the elevator, on the street, Joana apologized for not answering my question about a possible boyfriend. She said she was really worried, and that's why she seemed distracted and didn't answer my question. I don't know if that's true! There's something going on! **Based on Joana's friend's account, the group should outline Joana's profile based on her traits and characteristics.**

Text 3. Joana, the Mysterious One
My name's Arthur. I live in the same building as Paula, Joana's friend. I'm an honest and hardworking person. I don't have a girlfriend at the moment. To tell you the truth, I'm really into Joana, but apparently, she's not into me. Today I followed her to several places. First, she disappeared into the office where she works. I waited. Around ten o'clock she left alone. When she was a little way from the company building, she took out her cell phone and started to call someone. I heard her saying, *Don't do that, I'll drop by, and we'll talk about it* (...) *We'll get through this ... I'm on your side, ok.* You couldn't tell who she was talking to, but you could tell that Joana's getting involved with someone. Women get all flustered when they have a secret love affair. Maybe the guy's married. I went to the same restaurant Joana goes to for lunch. She gulped her food down and left. I waited a bit and followed her. She went into an old, dilapidated office building, very close to *Arouche*. I didn't hesitate and followed her! She went into a room that looked like a lawyer's office on the third floor. Through the window in the door, I saw her sitting at the desk, showing off her knees. Every now and then she would stroke an older man's hair. I couldn't catch what they were talking about. I felt sorry for her because there might be drugs involved, considering that place isn't genuinely nice. I was angry too, because she's nobody's fool. **Based on Arthur's account, the group should outline Joana's profile based on her traits and characteristics.**

Text 4. Joana, My Secretary
I'm the director of the sector where Joana works. For the third time this week she asked me if she could pop out quickly between ten and eleven o'clock. I can't complain about her work, so I let her. If she asks again, I will have to have a word with her. I've noticed that she's been sad lately. When I arrived, I asked her if everything was ok, and she said yes, thanking me for my concern. I notice that when it is near the end of the day, Joana is always looking at the clock. I don't know if she has anything urgent to do or if she wants to avoid leaving with someone from the office. **Based on Joana's boss's account, the group should outline Joana's profile based on her traits and characteristics.**

Text 5. Joana, My Boss
I'm an office assistant and I work for Joana. Other secretaries let me joke around, but she won't have it. She asked me to do her a favor today. She gave me a package to deliver near *Largo do Arouche* and paid me for it. She didn't need to, because it was on my way anyway. I don't know what was in that package. It was so tightly closed that you couldn't tell. I made the delivery and then told her that the person who received it didn't say a word, but he seemed on edge. He practically yanked the package out my hands. She looked pensive and smiled at me. She's got a nice smile, but I don't know, like, kind of sly. **Based on the office assistant's report, the group should outline Joana's profile based on her traits and characteristics.**

Text 6. Joana, My Customer
I work in a restaurant near the old center in São Paulo. The restaurant has a discount program with various companies. I know everyone well, because I listen to their conversations, I watch people's reactions, and lots of people tell me things. A waiter could be a good informant to the police. I've known Joana for over a year. I know she lives alone with her mother; she works and studies. What catches my eye is that she doesn't eat much. I'm sure it's not a diet she's on. She also seems nervous; maybe she's sleeping badly. Recently an older man came looking for her at lunchtime. I heard him say that he wouldn't stay because he didn't want to mess up her life. She insisted with him a lot, asking him to stay, and when he started to leave, she stopped eating her lunch and went with him. After that day, Joan has been reserved. Today she had lunch here, ate less than other times and left in a hurry. Then a boy called Arthur followed her out. I think they'd arranged some secret meeting, away from the restaurant. I just don't know where the other person stands in this story. **Based on the waiter's report, the group should outline Joana's characteristic profile.**

Text 7. Joana Herself

I live with my mother. We have a simple but spacious apartment. I work in an export company, and I'm a secretary in the overseas contacts department, thanks to my skills with English and Spanish. When I was a little girl, my mom told me that my dad went to Italy, disappearing from our lives. My mother and I didn't talk about him much; we assumed him as dead. A month ago, he reappeared. Our first meeting was surprising and took place in the restaurant where the company has a discount program. This turned my whole life upside down. My dad had located me through the help of his friend, who is a lawyer and has an office in *Largo do Arouche*. It's in this person's room that I have been meeting with him. My biggest concern is to prepare him and my mother to talk to each other after all this time. Of course, they have a lot to say to each other. It was difficult for me to accept him, and I imagine it'll be even more complicated for my mom. I've been trying to convince him to come see her for a long time. I intend to speak with her only after he agrees to it. I sent him a package with photos of the three of us to get him to consider the idea. The office assistant who delivered the package to him tried to find out what was it in, but I just smiled at him. I know a lot of people think that I am acting strangely, but I can't tell them anything, at least not now. Today was an important day. I had breakfast quickly, trying to appear calm. My mom gave me some advice. Soon after, I went to Marina's apartment, and I had to apologize to her because I wasn't paying attention to what she was saying. Then, at the company, my director let me leave. When I was in the street, I called my dad to find out about the photos. He was very emotional, and I managed to tell him that I would be on his side at this difficult time. I had lunch quickly, pretending not to notice the waiter staring at me curiously. He is always nice to me. I ran to the lawyer's office from the restaurant. I thought I saw Arthur hanging around. He seems interested in me, pity that he's not a very reliable person. When I met my dad I thought he was very sad, and I tried to cheer him up. For the first time, I was able to be affectionate with him, I ran my hand through his hair, which is already gray. I am very hopeful that everything will turn out ok.

Procedure

In preparation for the experiential activities, the facilitator should study the supporting text presented in the Material section.

The therapist should not make any comments about the content of *Joana's Story*. He/she only explains that the experiential activity will be divided into two phases. In the first phase, he/she divides the class into six groups, with four or five participants each. He/she gives each group the text with its corresponding number followed by the instruction to (a) choose one of the group members to coordinate the discussion of the content of the text; (b) write on a blank sheet of paper the number of the group (G1, G2, etc.), the names of the coordinator, spokesperson, and the other members; (c) silently read the text received; and (d) discuss and write on the sheet of paper what kind of person is being described.

Set approximately 20 min to complete this part of the work. During this activity, the facilitator monitors the groups, helping them while avoiding influencing the answers and, especially, supporting the roles of the coordinator and the spokesperson.

After the time is up, the facilitator explains that, in a moment, each group will be asked to read their text out loud and explain their interpretation about Joana and that the others should listen, as each group's text and the interpretation can bring additional elements to the analysis they themselves have made.

The facilitator writes the groups' numbers on the board. Then, goes on to the next stage, following a sequence of steps:

- He/she asks Group 1 to read their text and share their interpretation (monitoring the others so they only listen, without starting parallel conversations or reacting too openly).
- He/she says to the others, *Does any group want to change the interpretation they made based on Group One's analysis?* He/she waits a little while and then writes on the board, next to each group's number, YES, for those who changed their interpretation (and nothing if the answer is NO).
- He/she asks Group 2 to read their text and share their interpretation (monitoring the others so they only listen, without starting parallel conversations or reacting too openly).
- He/she asks the others again if they would change and writes YES next to the group's that say they would.

The facilitator proceeds in the same way with all the groups. In the case of those who indicated change, the facilitator should ask them to describe what changes were made to their analysis and why. After every group has given their accounts, the facilitator reads the last text (Joana herself) or asks someone in the group to do it. In general, people are often surprised by the text.

At this point, the facilitator gives the following instruction: *The texts that you received contained descriptive passages (facts) and interpretative passages (judgments). Each group must now identify in the text that they have analyzed what the facts are and what the judgments are.* If necessary, the facilitator explains in more detail what is an observable fact and what is the interpretation of a fact. The facilitator gives them a few minutes for the task and asks each group (not necessarily in the same sequence) to report the facts and interpretations. For the other groups, the facilitator asks them to confirm or disagree, if this is the case. Finally, he/she discusses the experiential activity with the groups, based on the following questions:

- *What are Joana's positive and negative aspects?*
- *Were the analyses that made up the profile you created for Joana based on facts or judgments?*
- *What happens on a day-to-day basis when we mistake judgments for facts? What are the consequences of this?*

- *How is it possible to change the harmful effects of this practice?*

At the end of the activity, the facilitator gives a short presentation based on the facilitator's supporting text (see Material).

Observations

- If the group is very large, the facilitator should consider the possibility of forming small groups with six participants or create one or two more groups, repeating texts five and six with them. Comparing different analyses of the same texts can greatly enrich the experiential activity.
- Often the groups' analyses, especially those working with texts, two, three, five, and six, may show negative prejudices. In this case, the facilitator should not disapprove but use this content to reflect on how often we make negative judgments and also let ourselves be influenced by judgments that are made with little or no grounding.
- If no prejudiced analysis of Joana appears, the facilitator should congratulate the groups and lead a discussion on negative judgments that may influence us. He/she should give examples of our prejudices about immigrants, refugees, gypsies, the poor, black people, etc. It explains that many of these negative biases are disguised. For example, in soap operas the roles of cleaners and criminals were given to black actors/actresses; Jews were given the roles of knickknack sellers, etc.

Variations

- Text 7 – Joan herself – can also be given to one group, adopting the same procedure in relation to the others.

10.2.17 What Can We Learn from Geese?

Objectives

- Specific

  Understand and value teamwork.
  Identify social skills important for teamwork (e.g., agreeing, disagreeing, asking questions, giving feedback, praising).
  Recognize the importance of variability in group work.
  Express empathy.
  Public speaking.
  Give feedback.

- Complementary

  Identify values underlying metaphors.
  Reflect on the various positions people are asked to fulfil in life.
  Participate in different tasks in the group.

Material

- Supporting text

What Can We Learn from Geese?
In some countries, in the fall, you can often see flocks of geese flying south. The organization of the flight calls our attention, as it is in the formation that resembles the letter V in an inverted position. This form is adopted because it helps the birds save a lot of energy on the long journey. Each bird, by flapping its wings, produces a vacuum that considerably reduces the resistance to the one immediately behind and so on. This encourages them to keep together, since trying to make the trip alone is more difficult given the greater effort required. In addition, the honking birds that fly at the back seem to encourage those in the front, but when those who are ahead get tired, they change positions with those that at the back. It is estimated that this formation saves about 70% of the energy used in the flight, considering another positioning. This does not mean that the journey is easy. Strong winds may force them to interrupt the flight, a tactic which avoids the flock dispersing. Other problems are injuries caused by unexpected crashes or hunters' shots. When a bird is injured or sick and leaves the flock, it is immediately surrounded by two geese, who try to help it. They accompany the bird until it recovers, or, in case of disability, they leave it and return to the group to continue the journey.

- Supporting questions for reflection.

  1. *Am I working isolated from other people?*
  2. *Does my behavior take into account the other people who make this "flight of life" with me?*
  3. *Have I been supportive to those who, due to some problem, leave the designated route somewhere along the way?*
  4. *Do I allow and even encourage others to take turns with me to lead the group?*
  5. *When I am not leading, have I encouraged my colleagues who are leading to conduct their tasks well?*
  6. *What does it mean to work in a group?*

7. *Is it possible to cultivate solidarity in the workplace?*
8. *Note down some difficulties of group work.*

Procedure

The facilitator distributes a copy of the supporting text *What we can learn from geese*? to everyone. He/she organizes the participants into groups, preferably formed by colleagues who have not yet worked together. The facilitator gives them 10 to 15 min to read the text silently and then discusses the possible lessons the text brings, jotting them down on a separate sheet.

After this phase, he/she asks each group to present their work, being careful to notice the groups that have reached similar results, if only in some aspects.

Then the facilitator hands out supporting text 2, asking them to read the items. He/she chooses one of the groups and asks, without further explanation, to think together for 3 min and come up with a way to act out question 3. The facilitator closely monitors the behavior of the group, giving positive feedback for skills such as cooperating, demonstrating empathy, agreeing/disagreeing, and making suggestions. He/she then draws everyone's attention to the group's presentation of the question, gives positive feedback, and introduces a participant from another group, giving this person instructions to question the group's behavior.

This procedure can be repeated with another group and another item. At the end, he/she checks what each group has learned from the experiential activity and asks for feedback from one group to another, monitoring the quality of the feedback and eventually giving feedback.

Observations

- This experiential activity focuses on values that should be highlighted by the facilitator.
- The values focused upon in this experiential activity are pertinent to various social situations at work, family, and school, among others.

Variations

- The facilitator can start with supporting text 2 and, after the group answers, the facilitator gives them supporting text 1 and asks them to review the previous answers.

10.2.18 *Hot and Cold*

Objectives

- Specific

  Discriminate simple verbal cues in social interaction situations.
  Make choices between two conflicting directions.
  Communicate and collaborate with partner.

- Complementary

  Give feedback.
  Praise the colleague who does the task well.

Material

- Small objects such as a handkerchief, a hair clip, a book
- Supporting text

About "Hot and Cold" Children's Play
This experiential activity has the same name as the traditional game: *Hot and Cold!* It was very common in the days when there was no television or electronic games. The game is most appropriate for children between 5 and 11 years but may also include teenagers. It can be played by two people; however, it is more interesting with a larger group. The rules are simple and include a leader, who can be a child or even an adult, and those who will look for a hidden object. These roles can be alternated. It is up to the leader to gather the group together, explain how the game works (if the others do not know) and lead it, asking them to choose someone to look for the object. The leader chooses and hides the object and gives some clues: *Hot!* or *Cold!* These words are said when the person who is looking for the object gets near or far away from the hidden object. Sometimes the leader can say different words such as *hot*, *boiling*, *on fire* or *cold*, *very cold*, and *freezing* to challenge the players.

Procedure

The facilitator explains to the client and the others (mother, sibling, colleagues), how to play the game (Hot and Cold). He/she checks if they know the game. Even if they know the game, he/she explains it quickly. He/she shows everyone the objects. Then, the facilitator tells them they need to pay attention, because the one who was picked to find the hidden object will have to move away from where they currently are when the clue is *Cold*. And when the clue is *Hot*, the object is nearby, and they have to look for the object.

If the therapist needs a model, a child with a good repertoire can be chosen. The therapist instructs everyone so that the model receives, after locating the object, some positive consequences, such as clapping, praise, comments, questions about how he/she found it, etc. After the model's turn, the client is asked to participate. The difficulty of the hiding place must be related to their capacities, keeping in mind that the difficulty will be increased after the first two times they got it right.

On the third attempt, a precondition can be introduced. Something like the participant needs to estimate the time it will take to find the object, or, after solving the problem, they must choose someone from the group to compliment them.

Observation

- This experiential activity can be done with children at school. In both cases, in group and individual intervention, the therapist can include the following as tasks: (a) invite a friend to talk or play with; (b) accept someone's invitation to play a game, etc.

Variations

- A variation that requires more specific clues, in addition to Cold or Hot, is to blindfold the participant, so he/she will have to use touch and hearing, and the leader will need to give more detailed clues.
- Another interesting variation is to search for the object in pairs and to alternate the clues, sometimes directed at one or the other member of the pair, so that they need to communicate with each other, discuss, evaluate, and decide together.

10.3 Examples of Analysis and Practice Exercises

10.3.1 Opting for Empathy

Objectives

- Specific

  Identify demands for different skills according to the situations.
  Understand the concept of empathy.
  Differentiate empathic from proto-empathic skills.
  Suggest empathic alternatives.

- Complementary

  Make choices as a group.
  Give feedback.

Material

- Card with a chart summarizing the characteristics that differentiate genuinely empathic behaviors from those who are considered to be proto-empathic and non-empathic (see Del Prette & Del Prette, 2001, p.89)
- Cards or strips of paper (numbered) with situations for practicing the empathic alternative (Table 10.4)

Procedure

The facilitator briefly discusses the importance of empathy in interpersonal relationships. He/she gives some examples and highlights the basic components of empathy: (a) listening carefully to someone, avoiding interrupting them; (b) putting yourself in someone else's shoes, trying to understand the situation he/she is going through; and (c) expressing this understanding in a discreet but active way. He/she remembers that empathy is not only a human ability, but it also appears in other animals, including in interactions between species. They should clarify that empathy has a genetic basis that may or may not consolidate depending on the conditions of the environment. The facilitator should also reaffirm that empathy can be learned, especially when the person is motivated to do so.

After this brief presentation, the facilitator organizes groups of three to five participants (depending on the number of participants). He/she gives each group two or three sets of situations. He/she asks each group to choose a coordinator to conduct the analysis of the material and a spokesperson to note the points of discussion.

The facilitator explains that each group should choose the alternative that they understand as more empathic to each situation and gives some time (which may vary in length depending on how advanced the groups are) for the task. When they have finished, he/she asks each group, through its coordinator, to read the situation and the alternatives for all the others, adopting the (relevant) nonverbal and paralinguistic patterns in the case of the empathic alternative. He/she asks them to explain which alternative they considered more empathetic and to justify their choice. He/she asks the other participants whether they agree or not and why. He/she can also ask the others to evaluate the suitability of these behaviors.

When the participants read the alternatives, the facilitator should value everyone's responses, highlight with positive feedback those that are consistent with the concept of empathy, and encourage reflection by asking questions, accepting opposing positions, while maintaining the concept of empathy. At the end, he/she sum-

Table 10.4 Practicing the emphatic alternative

SITUATION	REACTION A	REACTION B
1. A friend recounts, with difficulty, the breakup of a relationship.	*I understand how difficult this whole situation has been …*	*In a while you will not even remember how much you cried because of this break up.*
2. Your child is really scared about getting a recommended vaccine.	*It hurts a little at the moment, but then you won't get measles … Your Dad (Your Mum) is here with you …*	*You won't get measles after having the vaccine. Come on, stop whining, you're brave. If you're brave you won't feel the pain!*
3. Your brother-in-law drops by your house Saturday morning inviting you to see the new car he bought.	*Nice!!! This model is really great. I think you chose well!!! …*	*Cool … This model is great. However, it's the most sought after by thieves …*
4. I didn't pass the university entrance exam … The whole year I spent most of my time studying while many friends went to the movies, parties, bars, I gave my all... I worked so hard! I can't believe it!	*Look, Alex, you're still so young! That's life! You can do it again next year.*	*I know how hard it is for you, Alex. Even though I don't see you very often, I know from your parents how hard you worked!*
5. Vera!!! I have to tell you something. You won't believe it! You know that new position that was created in the company I work for? You are now talking to the PERSON IN CHARGE OF THE NEW SYSTEM!	*Great! Incredible, my friend! I'm really happy for you!*	*You see! And you were down in the dumps! It's like they say, God is on your side!*

continued

Table 10.4 (continued)

6. I'm confused! Whenever I see Paul, I'm happy. On the other hand, when I see Andrew, my heart races. I can´t like two guys that much at the same time. I think I'm fickle and I that worries me...	*I understand your situation, Helena. I think it's possible to like two people, especially given that Paul and Andrew are such nice guys ... If you want, we can talk about it...*	*Actually, Helena, I don´t think you like either of them. The same thing happened to me... Remember, last year ...*
7. I need to tell you all something that´s happening ... I'm afraid of losing my patience with the things Patrick does... If I go to the meeting I´ll just get upset, if I don´t go, it will make no difference. The other day...	*I know how you feel, but you have to react. There is no reason to feel so irritated. You have to take it in your stride. This shows your lack of self-confidence. I recommend you go speak to a psychologist.*	*Look, I think it's natural that you get annoyed, some jokes are not easy to swallow. Some people around us are more difficult to deal with. I think it was a good idea for you to talk about this with the group*

Note: The empathic responses are: 1A, 2A, 3B, 4B, 5A, 6A, 7B

marizes the responses consistent with the concept of empathy, discussing the difference between *proto-empathic* and truly empathic reactions.

Observations

- It is important to remember that empathy does not depend only on the topography of the response and that, although it is important, it is even more authentic in terms of social competence criteria, for example, (a) emotional expression with the other; (b) self-control and exercising patience to listen, without interrupting the interlocutor; and (c) helping the others develop possible solutions through listening, feedback, and, if appropriate, asking questions.
- The chart differentiating empathic, proto-empathic, and non-empathic responses can be presented and discussed before or at the end of the experience.

10.3.2 *Practicing Assertive Responses*

Objectives

- Specific

  Recognize situations that require assertive coping.
  Differentiate assertive, passive, and aggressive responses.
  Elaborate assertive responses to the situation.
  Recognize different assertive alternatives for the same situation.

- Complementary

  Predict likely results of assertive, passive, and aggressive responses to the same situation.
  Justify the choice for assertive alternatives in the analyzed situations.
  Develop self-monitoring.

Material

- Text on assertiveness, aggressiveness, and passivity (see Del Prette & Del Prette, 1999, pp. 40–44 and Del Prette & Del Prette, 2001, pp. 41–53)
- ACTIVITY CARDS, containing the outline of the proposed problem and the task requested of the group (Table 10.5)

Procedure

The facilitator says that everyone will participate in this experiential activity and writes on the board the terms: PASSIVITY, AGGRESSIVENESS, and ASSERTIVITY. He/she asks the participants what the meaning of each of these words is or to give examples of them in interpersonal relationships. In general, the terms passivity and aggressiveness are easily exemplified, and, in this case, the facilitator talks more about assertiveness, explaining its main characteristics.

Then the facilitator hands out the ACTIVITY CARD, explaining what is expected of each group. If the alternative produced by the group is not considered assertive by the others, the facilitator may ask them to make suggestions to improve it but highlighting the need to consider the social competence criteria. At a more advanced stage, the facilitator can and should also say that an assertive response is preceded by some expression of empathy.

Table 10.5 Practicing assertive alternative

Create a socially more competent (assertive) alternative to deal with the situation and act it out in front of the group.	
Group 1. You have been approached several times by someone who wants to sell you magazine subscriptions. He contacts you again, with the same proposal. You say:	
This is the third time you' ve called. *I've already told you* that I'm not going to buy any subscriptions. I'll call you if I change my mind.	
Group 2. A colleague asks you for a ride home. This is inconvenient because you are late, you have other things to do and a change in the route, at that moment, would be very bad. You (with discouraged expression) say:	
It's just that .... ok then! Let's go. I'll work it out.	
Group 3. You are the only woman in a work group who always ask you to be the secretary. You say:	
No!!! I'm tired and fed up of being the secretary. You force this task on me just because I'm the only woman in the group. Don't start!	
Group 4. Someone from the library calls and asks you to return a book you never borrowed. You answer:	
What are you talking about? You should control your records better! I never borrowed this book and it is unacceptable that you accuse me of this.	
Group 5. You're heading toward the photocopier when a colleague, who usually asks for help, including for xeroxing materials, asks you where you're going. You answer:	
I'm going to the cinema (in an ironic tone). Where do you think I'm going at this time of day!	
Group 6. A friend arrives very happily showing you her new dress she has bought and is wearing. You think the dress doesn't suit her. She says: It's so beautiful, isn't it? You...	
Mmm...It is beautiful. I´m glad you´re happy with it!	

Observation

- This experiential activity has two tasks. Depending on the group and the time available, they can be performed in different sessions, but it is recommended that they be consecutive.
- It is important for the groups to listen carefully to the presentation of each of the other groups. The strategy of asking them to provide feedback ends up getting the others to pay more attention.
- The fact that each group receives different situations for analysis broadens the spectrum of assertive possibilities to be learned by all participants.
- Some assertive responses can be understood by some (or by all) participants as aggressive. In this case, the facilitator clarifies that the criterion for differentiating assertiveness from aggression should be the evaluation of the group, of the subculture in which the individual is inserted, taking into account the instrumental and ethical dimensions of social competence and emphasizing (see Chap. 1) (a) the diversity of alternatives that can be assertive for the same situation (behavioral variability) and (b) choose the level of assertiveness, that is, the need to match the force of confrontation according to the severity of demand. In this case, it is important to give additional examples.
- It is also important to clarify that sometimes the classification of a behavior as assertive or aggressive may depend on the topography (nonverbal and paralinguistic components). For example, when telling the other person *I can't help you right at this moment*, this reaction may be considered aggressive if the person speaks louder than necessary, frowns, or stares. On the other hand, he/she can be understood as assertive if they speak in a firm voice, looking at the interlocutor, with a facial expression that shows the end of the subject.

Variations

- Hand out strips of paper with just the situation, requesting that each group complete it by writing down an assertive response. Then, ask the groups to read the prepared response and ask another group to assess whether the response can be considered assertive or not.
- One can also request participants to analyze texts from well-known novelists who created stories where the character showed difficulties in assertiveness. An example is Anton Tchekhov's short story, *The Fool: A Failed Business and Other Short Stories* (São Paulo: L&PM Editors).
- This experiential activity can take place before or after analyzing movies that portray demands for assertiveness, such as *Amanha Nunca Mais* (a Brazilian movie) and *The Man Next Door*, all with excellent passages for analysis not only of the assertive, passive, and aggressive attitudes but also of the associated contingencies, especially the consequences of these behaviors in the daily life of the characters.

References

Del Prette, Z. A. P., & Del Prette, A. (1999). *Psicologia das Habilidades Sociais: Terapia, Educação e Trabalho [The Psychology of Social Skills: Therapy, Education and Work]* (1st. ed.). Petrópolis (SP): Vozes.

Del Prette, A., & Del Prette, Z. A. P. (2001). *Psicologia das relações interpessoais e habilidades sociais: Vivências para o trabalho em grupo [The psychology of interpersonal relationships and social skills: Experiential activities for groups]* (1st ed.). Petrópolis, Brazil: Vozes.

Index

Z. A. P. Del Prette, A. Del Prette, *Social Competence and Social Skills*,
https://doi.org/10.1007/978-3-030-70127-7

S

The manufacturer's authorised representative in the EU is Springer
Nature Customer Service Centre GmbH, Europaplatz 3, 69115 Heidelberg,
Germany. If you have any concerns regarding our products, please
contact ProductSafety@springernature.com

Printed and bound by CPI Group (UK) Ltd, Croydon, CR0 4YY
30/09/2026
02225694-0001